THE **GOLDILOCKS** PARADOX

The Goldilocks Paradox

Interoception, Stress Mastery, and the Key to Thriving in Complexity

Colleen Mizuki

Published by Game Changer Publishing

Paperback ISBN: 979-8-90158-202-2

Hardcover ISBN: 979-8-90158-062-2

Digital ISBN: 979-8-90158-063-9

www.GameChangerPublishing.com

To my extraordinary daughter, Maya,
who has inspired me from day one
to embody love, compassion, and authenticity.

Advance Praise for The Goldilocks Paradox

"*The Goldilocks Paradox* is an invaluable guide for individuals looking to transform stress into a positive force that sustains high performance and supports both mental and physical well-being. While serving as a U.S. Ambassador at high-threat overseas posts, I recognized the importance of maintaining mind-body equilibrium. I just didn't know there was a name for it (interoceptive awareness) and that this could be cultivated intentionally. Drawing on science, data, and real-world examples, Colleen Mizuki explains how interoceptive awareness skills help people leverage stress for sustained high performance and overall well-being. Packed with valuable information and practical insights, *The Goldilocks Paradox* is an ideal resource for anyone eager to strengthen their mind-body connection and learn how to make stress work for them."

— Lisa A. Johnson, U.S. Ambassador (ret.)

"No one these days—whatever our roles in life—is immune from the effects of stress and wouldn't like to modulate it better. Colleen Mizuki invites us to consider a technique in which she has developed expertise that cannot eliminate stress but can help us deal with it better."

— Bob Gersony, Humanitarian Field Worker

"As both a soldier and a police officer, I've faced the kind of pressure that tests your limits physically, mentally, and emotionally. Colleen Mizuki's work cuts straight to the heart of what it means to perform under extreme stress. Her insights are not only grounded in research but also offer a deep understanding of the real-world challenges faced by those of us in high-stakes professions. This book is more than guidance; it's a lifeline. Colleen gives voice to the struggles we often carry in silence and provides tools that can truly make a difference. Anyone working in a high-stress arena, in uniform or otherwise, needs to read this."

— Tom Deluccia, Police Officer LAPD Bomb Squad/Major U.S. Army

"Drawing on years of experience working with leaders under intense pressure, Colleen Mizuki offers a clear, science-based roadmap for mastering stress and sustaining performance. *The Goldilocks Paradox* is essential reading for any leader, particularly those leading teams across cultures and high-stakes environments."

— David Livermore, PhD, Bestselling Author on Leadership & Cultural Intelligence

"As someone who's spent years pushing my body and mind to their limits, I found this book incredibly pertinent. Colleen gets what it means to face pressure, setbacks, and the constant need to show up at your best. Her take on resilience and interoceptive awareness—really learning to listen to what's happening inside—has given me a whole new perspective on performance and recovery, both on and off the field. It's more than a book about performance and well-being, though. It's a guide to, as Colleen says, 'doing life better.'"

— Ben Foster, Former Professional Sportsperson

"Colleen Mizuki offers a refreshing perspective on performance improvement that leverages interoception (bodily awareness) to achieve success and well-being. Her practical and science-based insights make *The Goldilocks Paradox* a must-read for anyone seeking to be effective while thriving."

— Jenny Baker, Former Senior VP for Business Optimization at DAI Global

"After two decades in uniform, I've seen firsthand that pressure isn't the enemy—losing touch with our internal signals is. In the military, we're trained to stay composed but not always taught how to understand what's happening inside when stress climbs. *The Goldilocks*

Paradox provides a grounded, accessible path to reading those internal cues and responding with clarity. Colleen Mizuki bridges the science of human performance with the realities of high-pressure leadership in a way every leader can use."

— Anh Ky Ban, U.S. Army

"*The Goldilocks Paradox* is a powerful reminder that true resilience isn't about pushing harder; it's about listening inward. Colleen Mizuki shows how interoceptive awareness can help us thrive with balance, curiosity, and connection, even in high-stress worlds."

— Dr. Kelly Mahler, OTD, Occupational Therapist and Author of *The Interoception Curriculum*

"Everyone tells me to listen to my body. Colleen tells me why and how this is done. Read this book. Your overwhelmed brain will thank you for it."

— Zena Everett, Author of *The Crazy Busy Cure* and *Badly Behaved People*

"I first worked with Colleen in the resilience space more than a decade ago, and her forward-looking insights remain unparalleled to this day. She has helped so many people. I strongly endorse her book."

— Robert Skidmore, Director of Operations and Finance, Cheetah Conservation Fund

"This book changed how I understand performance under pressure. Colleen reveals that resilience doesn't come from pushing harder, but it comes from noticing stress early and modulating it skillfully. Her insights made me rethink how I lead, recover, and decide. Her approach turns stress mastery into a framework enabling sustainable innovation and smarter growth for leaders and teams under pressure."

— Chang-Kyu Kim, Entrepreneur and Global Strategy Advisor in high-stakes innovation and cybersecurity

"Oh, you'll want to read this! Thorough, insightful, and absolutely useful, this book shows how tuning into the body strengthens the mind and empowers new possibilities. It's essential reading for resilience in a chaotic world."

— Kelly Corbet, Author of *Already Here: The Matter of Love*, and *BIG: The Practice of Joy*.

Read This First

As a thank you for buying and reading my book, scan the QR code below to access free interoceptive awareness resources or schedule a complimentary call to learn more!

Scan the QR Code Here:

THE **GOLDILOCKS** PARADOX

INTEROCEPTION, STRESS MASTERY, AND THE KEY TO THRIVING IN COMPLEXITY

COLLEEN MIZUKI

Foreword

In elite sport, we are taught to push, to override discomfort, to ignore the body's quieter messages, and to keep going long after our reserves should have told us to stop. I used to believe that resilience was about grit, determination, pushing your limits, and bouncing back from adversity. While that mindset carried me a long way, it came with a cost.

I learned the hard way. Relentless, laser-focused mindset and pursuit of excellence had taken me to world-class performance. But eventually, my body said NO, and it stopped working.

For three years, I battled symptoms that neither my medical team nor I could make sense of. I was ultra-professional and rigorous with every aspect of rest and recovery. Nutrition, physiotherapy, soft tissue work, psychology, optimizing my sleep, daily ice baths, compression wear, you name it, I treated it as a non-negotiable. I followed a tailored training program designed specifically for my needs. My support team and I were leaving no stone unturned, or so we thought.

Still, my legs would burn like fire. At times, it felt as though my body had been poisoned. My legs grew heavy, like lead, far from ideal for an elite athlete. My mental health struggled. I became frustrated, irritable, and increasingly disconnected from myself and others. My mind felt scattered, foggy, and weighed down. Training at my usual intensity became a battle, and my performance on the track began to nosedive. The stress and pressure to perform only intensified under the scrutiny of a high-performance, medal-winning system and the media.

So, I did what I knew best: I dedicated myself even more. I pushed harder. Ignored the symptoms. Hoped they would disappear as suddenly as they had arrived.

But after a long search for answers, everything shifted. Once I realized what was actually happening and listened to the intelligence of my own internal signals, the symptoms never returned. I went on to compete at a world-class level for a further 13 years.

At the time, I had no idea that those signals were trying to guide me, not hinder me. I just needed to learn how to listen and respond.

Along my journey as an Executive High Performance and Resilience Coach, I dug into the science and neurophysiology behind my experience and symptoms. Only then did I truly understand what had been missing and what had been the underlying cause all along.

Performance (real performance, sustainable performance) begins with the ability to notice, interpret, and respond wisely to our internal world. That capacity has a name: interoceptive awareness.

What Colleen Mizuki has done in this book is something rare. She has taken one of the most foundational human capacities, one that influences every aspect of resilience, well-being, and sustained-performance stress, and made it more accessible, practical, and deeply relevant to modern life. Whether you're leading a team, caring for others, navigating pressure, or simply trying to show up fully for the people you love, she explains how interoceptive awareness skills are transformative.

In sport, we often talk about "finding flow," that state where everything feels effortless and aligned. But flow is not magic. It's not luck. It's the outcome of a well-trained nervous system and a mind that listens to the body instead of battling it. Interoceptive awareness is the bridge that connects these systems, allowing us to perform at a high level without sacrificing our health, relationships, or sense of self.

Colleen's grasp of this subject is one of the most profound I've had the fortune of encountering in or outside elite sport. She brings together the science of stress physiology, the neurophysiology and psychology of resilience, and the wisdom of lived human experience. She also brings something just as important: compassion. She knows that most of us have been taught to override, suppress, or ignore what our bodies are trying to tell us. She knows the toll this takes. And she offers another way forward.

This book invites you to develop a skill I wish I had mastered much earlier in my career. It will introduce you to how you can recognize the early signs of overload before they become problems. It makes the argument on how interoceptive awareness strengthens our ability to stay grounded under pressure. It discusses how this capacity helps us access clarity, confidence, and presence—not by forcing ourselves to "try harder," but by learning how to work with the remarkable intelligence within our own body.

Whether you are an athlete, a leader, a parent, or someone simply trying to navigate an increasingly demanding world, the tools in these pages are for you.

May this book help you discover what I discovered late in my competitive years:

Resilience isn't built by pushing past your limits. It's built by learning how to listen.

Nathan Douglas
Double Olympian, Two-time European Medalist & Eight-time British Champion—Triple Jump
Executive High-Performance and Resilience Coach

Contents

Introduction

"It ain't what you don't know that gets you into trouble. It's what you know for sure that just ain't so."
—18th-century humorist Josh Billings (a Billings original and one of Mark Twain's favorite sayings)

What if high performance doesn't rely *only* on working longer hours or pushing harder?

What if the things we believe give us a performance edge might actually be eroding it?

What if we could enjoy longer-lasting high performance without risking burnout, damaged relationships, and compromised mental and physical health?

What if there were one single capacity, one we are born with but rarely develop fully, that is key to enjoying high performance without sacrificing the other areas of our lives?

High performance is not limited to executives, senior civil servants, special operations military, or world-class athletes. It is about the sustained ability of each of us to deliver our best results at any level and in any role.

Many people believe they are stuck with a hard choice: either achieve outstanding results at work and sacrifice other parts of their lives (relationships, physical health, and so on) *or* accept letting go of a desired performance outcome in order to enjoy well-being (mental and physical health, quality relationships, life satisfaction, etc.). While life is a series of trade-offs, this narrow, either/or construct about high performance versus well-being is a false dichotomy.

It's reasonable for us to attribute high performance to factors like hard work, long hours, intelligence or talent, technical expertise, and mental toughness. While such factors no doubt play an important role, they are not what will maintain high performance over the long haul without collateral damage.

It is not true that we have to choose *either* high performance *or* well-being. They are not opposing forces. Quite the opposite is true. Paradoxically, our ability to enjoy sustained high performance without sacrificing well-being relies to a large degree on how well we leverage stress as a source of usable energy. If we truly understand our stress from start to finish of a stress cycle, we can use it to fuel high performance and well-being.

A stressor is anything, whether internal (such as chronic pain, emotionally painful memories, fear of failure) or external (cancelled flight, interpersonal conflicts, deadlines, job insecurity, etc.), that throws our system out of balance. Stress is the brain-body system's process of mobilizing energy so we can respond and adapt to challenges (good, bad, or somewhere in between) and threats (real or perceived).

The trick is catching stress the moment it arises, knowing how to modulate it (dial it up and down) to a *just-right* level for the task and circumstance, and then adequately recovering from it. These skills of adaptively regulating stress strengthen resilience, which makes well-being and high performance compatible, not mutually exclusive.

Almost to a person, my clients initially define resilience to be "bouncing back" from challenges. While that is not quite accurate (resilience is more than just bouncing back, which we'll explore a bit later), most of them do understand the first part of the operating principle of resilience: that we need stress in order to be resilient. But they don't fully understand the rest. Few realize that we must be able to *fully* recover from it to gain resilience.

Even fewer know what full recovery actually feels like.

There is, however, a widely accessible example that helps explain the operating principle of resilience: weightlifting. Even the non-gym rat basically understands that increasing muscle mass requires stressing the muscles enough (creating micro tears) to stimulate growth, but that too much stress (stress that exceeds the body's recovery capacity) increases the risk of injury and burnout. In a nutshell, growth requires stress followed by adequate recovery for repair and adaptation.

Importantly, effective and efficient weightlifters know what this process *feels* like, from sensing in the muscles the right level of stress for growth without overdoing it and sensing when they have recovered. They *feel* the difference between productive strain and injury strain.

My mission is to help people have this level of understanding when it comes to stress, growth, and adaptability in their day-to-day lives. For this to happen, it's important to grasp this parallel, not just conceptually but in the body. Like effective weightlifters, it's crucial that we are able to *feel* our way through the stress cycle.

Fortunately, our brain-body system has a process, called **interoception,** that allows us to develop this ability. Interoception involves continuous communication between body and brain: the brain interprets bodily signals and makes adjustments to keep us balanced and functioning well. Importantly, interoception governs more than our physical functioning. It informs our perceptions, emotions, decisions, and actions; it underpins our cognitions (thinking) and attention. It also contributes to our empathy and social connection, in addition to other capacities.

I often describe interoception as an ongoing conversation between the brain and body. Metaphorically, the body is the speaker, communicating through messages such as heart rate, characteristics of breath, body temperature, gut signals, and more. In this sense, it provides meaning and structure, like a language's semantics and syntax. The brain is the listener, interpreting and responding in ways that keep us alive and functioning well. It is basically keeping the dialogue balanced and productive.

Just as we have the capacity to learn languages and become proficient, we can also learn how to consciously and productively engage in this brain-body conversation. The trainable dimension of interoception is called **interoceptive awareness**: our innate, though often underdeveloped, capacity to tune into (i.e., sense into the body or feel) and accurately interpret those bodily signals. This is crucial for resilience, which, as mentioned, is key to well-being and performance.

Interoceptive awareness plays such a critical role because it enables us to pick up on and interpret early stress signals in the body. When we are able to quickly detect bodily signs of a stress response and accurately assess them with practice, we are able to make conscious adjustments to that stress level, in essence, becoming an ally to what our brain is constantly trying to do. We can be like a force multiplier for the brain's ongoing effort to optimize our internal balance. By learning to speak the brain-body language, we are able to determine if the level of stress we're experiencing is *just right* for the situation and, with some basic techniques, dial this level up or down for situational needs and then efficiently and effectively recover. Extending the language metaphor, interoceptive awareness helps us upgrade the software of our language app.

This is not just a nice-to-have-if-we-have-time kind of thing. A growing body of research confirms that interoceptive awareness is key to resilience (Fermin et al. 2024; Grabbe, Duva, and Nicholson 2023; Solano Durán et al. 2024). It serves, in a sense, as a real-time internal feedback loop that enables adaptive stress regulation, which drives resilience, which in turn underpins well-being and sustained high performance. The best part is that interoceptive awareness can be trained and strengthened throughout our lives, and, even better, it doesn't take much time out of our busy days to build and strengthen. The bottom line is that developing interoceptive awareness offers a very good ROI.

I have worked with thousands of people from vastly different professions, missions, and countries. My clients come from the military, law enforcement, the diplomatic corps, humanitarian organizations, and firefighting teams. They educate our children, support teachers, or are taught by these dedicated educators. They entertain and expand our thinking through their writing, acting, and art. They inspire us with their athletic prowess and expressive grace on the field, pitch, court, or stage. They include foster parents and community volunteers, executives in large corporations, owners of small businesses, and employees who ensure those organizations run smoothly and meet company goals.

Several things have become very clear to me over the past two decades of working with so many people from various stages, walks of life, and cultures, being involved in research, and training people to increase their resilience and performance under stressful conditions. Out of all of this, I have come to the following conclusions: (1) We naturally desire a way to *do* life better (including but not limited to our jobs), feel more capable, and have meaningful connection with others; (2) The vast majority of us go through life only partially recovering from the onslaught of chronic stress such that being stressed-out feels *normal*; (3) Very few people know how to recognize the early signs of stress in order to modulate it for optimal benefit; and (4) We can all achieve greater resilience, performance, and well-being by sensing and acting on the signals that the body sends to the brain that enable us to effectively modulate our stress and reach full recovery.

I also find that many people are so accustomed to living in a high-stress state that they have become disconnected from their internal selves (no longer sensing what the body is telling them). As a result, any drop in their stress level is taken as recovery, when often it is not. Taking some downtime in the evening, or even a nice holiday, is not necessarily enough to fully recover from the stress they've accumulated. So, after the break, they aren't emerging stronger, more adaptable, and increasingly stress-hardy—the fundamental definition of resilience.

Disconnecting from our inner selves (bodily signals) causes us to lose touch with how to know whether or not we have fully recovered from a stressful experience and how to accurately gauge our resilience. Since the specific term "interoceptive awareness" is relatively new, there are no direct historical studies of where we stand right now versus in times past. Nonetheless, indirect evidence points to prior generations' lifestyles having naturally fostered a greater connection to internal body signals. Sensitivity to hunger, exhaustion, thirst, and emotional states was strengthened by daily physical effort, reliance on simpler and scarcer foods, exposure to the outdoors without contemporary temperature control, and a relative lack of continual external distractions.

Now, it seems likely that even if we do sense the need to rest, hydrate, eat, or move our bodies, our mind often tricks us into believing that we don't have time to stop to do this, that we'll be fine if we don't, or that the goal of the moment is more important than supporting our capacity to reach future goals (and so often our future goals, once we get to them, seem much more valuable than those from our earlier years!). Signals that scream for attention very often get pushed aside. Instead of heeding the signs our bodies and brains are sending, we pride ourselves on having grit or mental toughness, mistaking those for resilience, and charge on.

Modern living seems to have weakened our capacity to sense what our bodies are telling us and to interpret it accurately. Our fluency in understanding these internal cues is diminished by sedentary lifestyles, food availability, constant digital distractions, and the outsourcing of physical interpretation to medical systems or equipment, to name a few factors. Today's cross-cultural research confirms this trend: Communities influenced by contemporary industrial lifestyles tend to have lower levels of interoceptive awareness than those that incorporate activities like yoga, meditation, martial arts, or traditional medicine.

> It's not enough to attend a weekly yoga class and not think about the body's signals until the next class or meditate once a month. We need to make interoceptive awareness part of our existence, forming a habit to pause, listen to the body, and then choose how to meet the needs our system is expressing.

Although it appears that many, perhaps most, of us have diminished bandwidth to listen to the body, this does not imply that we are no longer capable. The brain circuitry that enables this capacity is still there, waiting to be activated. So, while it is underdeveloped, interoceptive awareness is still possible. It can be recovered and enhanced with intentional effort, allowing us to regain an innate human ability that was formerly necessary in day-to-day life.

This book is my invitation to engage your curiosity about what most fundamentally helps us function at our best and for the longest time possible, even under high-stress conditions. Using case studies, I illustrate real-life examples of what happens when leaders and teams are not able to modulate (dial up or down) their stress and when chronic stress becomes pervasive, throwing their balance off so far as to create dysfunction.

I will describe how I merged interoceptive awareness with other widely known techniques and approaches to bring about incredible change. Some of the case studies may seem a bit extreme, but my guess is that you will either see yourself (or, perhaps, shadows of yourself) or someone you know in these scenarios. I hope to instill in you the realization that even the most challenging situations can be improved when people take the time to tune in and recover.

I hope to impress upon you how interoceptive awareness skills open up opportunities to make wise and highly beneficial choices. I want to illustrate just how it provides us greater control over what we think, how we think, what we say, how we say it, what we eat, how we eat, when to rest, when to get up and stretch or move our bodies, and so much more. It offers us more power over our thoughts, choices, actions, and reactions. The source of such control is beautifully described in a quote that is widely attributed to Viktor Frankl, an Austrian neurologist, psychiatrist, philosopher, Holocaust survivor, and author of numerous books, including his influential book *Man's Search for Meaning*: "Between stimulus and response, there is a space. In that space is our power to choose our response. In our response lies our growth and our freedom."

What I value in this quote attributed to Dr. Frankl is the idea that we are not captive to all of our thoughts, moods, urges, and reactions. We have so many more choice points than we realize and more agency than we often exercise. Many people, if they were being honest, might say they feel just the opposite. They feel out of control with their thoughts, moods, impulses, cravings, urges, and reactions. This is to be expected if we rarely experience that crucial *space* between event (stimulus) and response. Interoceptive awareness helps us create and extend that space, giving ourselves even more time to choose the best way forward.

If you would like to *be* better in some way or *do* something better, I urge you to read this book. Even if you don't yet work in an office, have no desire for top leadership positions, or don't see yourself as a high performer, my guess is that you are always striving to do your best. While I use work-based case studies to illustrate the power inherent in interoceptive awareness skills, the stories describe human problems, not just business or organizational ones. The challenges and pitfalls illustrated apply to every one of us in any situation we're in because they stem from our system (brain-body) being out of kilter.

I've never met or worked with anyone who didn't want to do something better or be better at something, so I feel certain that anyone can find value in the message of this book. I suspect that every person on this earth would rather have more control over their stress, their reactions to stress, and the impact of that stress. We all have an innate drive, if not yet a developed curiosity, about how we might tap into our natural capacity to keep our systems healthier and more capable for a productive, meaningful life.

My experience working with thousands of people from vastly different fields and in various stages of life and career, all with similar issues related to stress and low interoceptive awareness, has led me to write this book. While the number of articles on interoception has gone up quickly in the past decade, few people are aware of the *trainable* dimension of this naturally occurring brain-body interaction that we can develop: interoceptive awareness.

The information in this book is designed to alert you to this powerful yet simple tool of interoceptive awareness, the basis of which you already have in your possession but is often out of your grasp. While this book is not written as a self-study in interoceptive awareness, I hope it will allow you to seek more information and guidance on building your interoceptive awareness and encouraging others to do so as well.

My goal is to make a case for the critical importance and high return on investment of listening closely to your body and tuning into the signals indicating your state, so you are able to be part of the crucial conversation between the body and the brain in their heroic attempts to keep us not just alive but moving toward thriving.

HOW THIS BOOK IS ORGANIZED

Chapter 1 is a quick but slightly extended discussion of the basic concepts and vocabulary introduced above. It sets the stage for an exploration of stress and resilience as a biological imperative of our brain-body system, of the role of interoceptive awareness in that imperative, and, ultimately, in our ability to sustain high performance without sacrificing well-being. This short chapter will, I hope, lay the foundation and stimulate your curiosity to do more.

Chapters 2 and 3 discuss stress. In Chapter 2, we dip our toes in, looking at real-life examples from participants in workshops of how chronic stress impacts us when we're not paying attention and why it is important to know if the level of stress in our system is *just right* for the task and situation at hand.

In Chapter 3, we immerse ourselves a little deeper into the topic of stress, exploring why we seem to be suffering the effects of stress more than past generations. I realize there are thousands of books on all aspects of stress (I've read them!), so my intention is to offer you a viewpoint that might evolve your understanding of what stress really is and how to make it work for you rather than against you. I have worked hard to keep these discussions at a fairly high level, offering just enough information to make the key points. I love the science of stress, resilience, interoception, and the trainable capacity of interoceptive awareness, but the scope of this book is designed to raise awareness and pique curiosity, not to explain every detail. I will also discuss three strategies and approaches for managing stress and how they complement each other.

Chapter 4 departs from stress to explore our various forms of intelligence and how interoceptive awareness affects these capacities. I included this chapter because (1) I've long been fascinated with the different frameworks and theories of intelligence and how the concept and definition have evolved, especially in recent decades, (2) it's highly valued by most people and an important ingredient for performance, and (3) I have found that most people don't realize how much stress (and, thus, resilience) plays a role in accessing our full range of intellectual capacities.

I love the science of stress, resilience, well-being, and performance, and I am fascinated by frameworks of intelligence, and you might be as well. I have tried to distill the essential and relevant elements of these topics in Chapters 1 through 4. If you would rather bypass these discussions, then jump right to the practical application of interoceptive awareness alongside other human-development tools described in the case studies.

Chapters 5 through 11 provide short descriptions of what can happen at an individual, team, and organizational level when stress is not modulated (and becomes a serious chronic issue) and how I helped them. These case studies provide examples of how coaching and training in interoceptive awareness support a healthier, more productive, and cohesive workplace and, when integrated skillfully into popular human-development models and frameworks, can lead to transformational shifts.

Please note that this book is designed to provide a basis for understanding the trainable elements of interoception (i.e., interoceptive awareness), why it is important to enhance our interoceptive awareness, and how to integrate this capacity into any human-development or professional-development approach. It is not designed as a step-by-step guide to building your interoceptive awareness. This capacity building is best done with the guidance of an expert, as the critical element is not limited to noticing bodily signals (which, for some, is already a significant challenge) but to accurately interpret those signals and know how to take effective and appropriate action based on that interpretation.

Interoceptive awareness involves becoming more aware of subtle, often unfamiliar internal cues, many of which are rooted in our built-in stress and recovery system (the autonomic nervous system, or ANS, which is explained in Chapters 1 and 2). It is easy to misread or misinterpret bodily signals, and it can be difficult to effectively fold this new skill into other performance and well-being improvement plans. Interoceptive awareness taps into our most basic biological functioning, so developing it effectively and safely calls for guidance from someone who helps tune into the signals, coaches in accurate interpretation, and supports the process of using this new information to make choices and decisions.

The science of interoception has grown in recent years, yet little has been written about the related trainable skill and capacity of interoceptive awareness. My goal for this book is to lay a foundation for better understanding this crucial skill and capacity and to provide examples of how it helps us in our everyday lives, from making better decisions and building more resilient teams to, ultimately, *doing life better*. My hope is that the information and case studies will pique your curiosity and inspire you to enhance your own interoceptive awareness and that of your team members. You will not be disappointed with the outcomes!

Chapter One

BASIC TERMS AND CONCEPTS RELATED TO INTEROCEPTIVE AWARENESS

"The limits of my language mean the limits of my world."
—Ludwig Wittgenstein (1889–1951),
Austrian philosopher of language and mind

KEY TAKEAWAYS:

- The autonomic nervous system, or ANS, is the part of our nervous system that controls life-sustaining functions, such as heart rate, breathing, and digestion (and many more). It governs our stress response and recovery, constantly adjusting energy, focus, and physiology to keep us balanced, like an accelerator (fight/flight) and brake pedal (rest/digest).
- For me, high performance extends beyond gold medals, corner offices, or top salaries. It is also about consistently bringing our best capacities (mental, physical, and emotional) to challenges in effective, ethical, and

energizing ways and, ideally, to further meaningful causes.

- Neurophysiological regulation is how the brain and body keep us in balance, and interoceptive awareness helps us notice and support that process.
- Stress mobilizes energy in the brain and body to help us meet life's demands, challenges (good, bad, or somewhere in between), or threats (real or perceived).
- The level of stress needed depends on many factors, such as how our nervous system is "wired" and "trained" (how easily it activates and recovers), and the type of task. High stress levels can help in routine, rehearsed, or manual tasks, while lower stress levels are generally best for highly complex tasks like creative thinking, problem solving, or collaboration with others.
- Stress "regulation" typically refers to interventions or strategies to down-regulate (i.e., reduce or recover from) stress. I use stress "modulation" to indicate that we may not always need to down-regulate (lower) our stress levels. Sometimes we need to upregulate it, injecting more stress into our system to optimize attention, focus, and performance. Modulating stress is like dialing it up and down as needed. Interoceptive awareness helps us know if we're at the optimal level of stress.
- Mindfulness and body-based therapies like Somatic Experiencing® are helpful in supporting our interoceptive awareness.

I believe that the words we choose matter, not just as reflections of how we see the world, but as forces that shape how we understand it. Linguists, psychologists, neuroscientists, and philosophers agree on the power of words to shape how we think and feel, influence our physiology, and expand or limit our mental experiences (Brooks et al. 2017, 169-183; Cui, Ren, and Zhou 2025). Because language shapes and describes our reality, it felt important to clarify how I use the terms *stress, resilience, well-being,* and *performance* in this book, and to invite you to reflect on how you understand them as well.

THE RELATIONSHIP BETWEEN STRESS AND PERFORMANCE

It makes sense to start with stress, since it's such a commonly used term. I find that just about everyone understands that stress is neither bad nor good. But, in everyday conversations, stress is typically described or alluded to as something unpleasant or unwanted. For me, this is an issue for the reasons mentioned above, namely that words both reflect and reinforce our beliefs. The underlying connotation of stress being unwanted is a limiting belief that can have an impact on our well-being and sustained performance. As the saying goes, perception is reality.

In fact, stress is neither good nor bad, and I find it very important for my clients to better understand stress as a concept and a reality, becoming familiar with how it shows up for each of them and learning how to adjust it to meet the demands of a situation. Leveling up this understanding and familiarity makes it much easier to work directly with the system that governs our stress response and recovery, the autonomic nervous system (ANS), and the intersection between brain and body.

This intersection is where interoceptive awareness lies. By seeing and correctly interpreting internal body signals, we take part in the ongoing dialogue between brain and body, influencing not only how experiences are perceived in the mind but also how patterns of brain activity are gradually calmed, rewired, or reinforced. It's the basis for so much of our capacity, from survival and adaptation to the many changes we experience, as well as resilience, well-being, and sustained high performance.

To set the stage for the discussions on stress in Chapters 2 and 3, it's important to note that I use a biological definition of stress, which is, simply put, *energy mobilized by the brain-body system (the "system") to allow us to respond to a challenging, demanding, or threatening event.* This is sometimes referred to as "stress arousal." I have found in my work that it's helpful to view stress on a spectrum from low to high arousal and to overlay that with "performance," meaning our ability to carry out tasks that are cognitive, physical, emotional, psychological, or social.

Below is a modification of the well-known illustration of the stress-to-performance relationship. This illustration goes by different names: the Yerkes-Dodson Law or the Inverted-U Curve (in scientific circles); the Stress-Performance Curve (a common term used in mindfulness coaching and other coaching contexts); and the Eustress Curve in teaching, training, and psychology and performance-centered discussions in sports, business/leadership training, the military, etc.

In Figure 1.1, I have adapted the Yerkes-Dodson concept to align with examples of possible interoceptive bodily signals and cognitive, psychological, and behavioral indicators of stress arousal (stress levels). Let's take a quick look at it here, and it will come up again in the final case study when we look at an important example of when it's necessary to increase our stress activation level to improve performance.

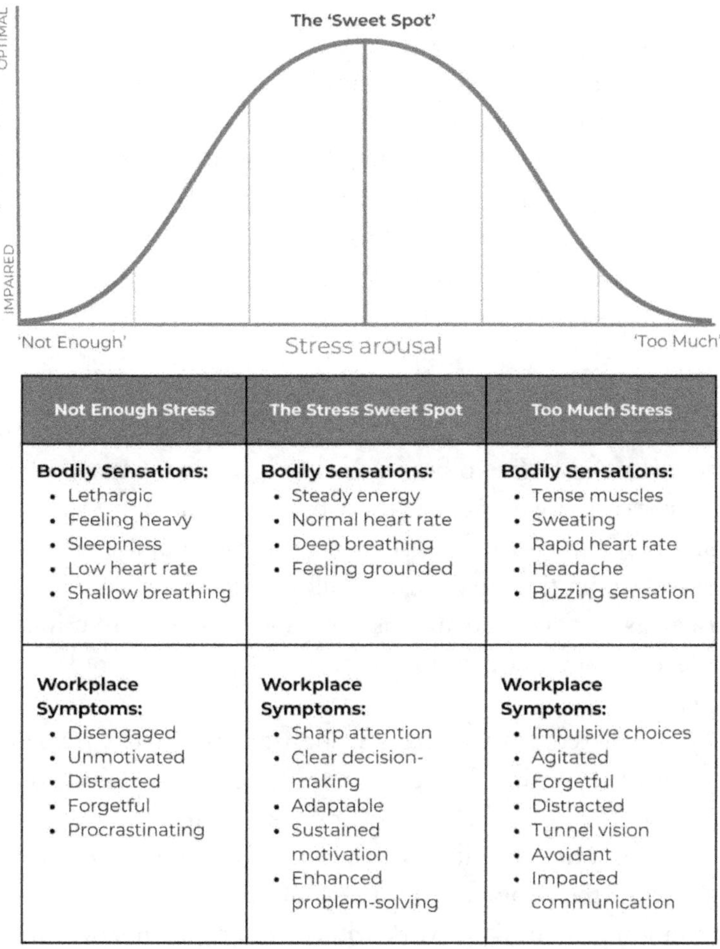

Not Enough Stress	The Stress Sweet Spot	Too Much Stress
Bodily Sensations: • Lethargic • Feeling heavy • Sleepiness • Low heart rate • Shallow breathing	**Bodily Sensations:** • Steady energy • Normal heart rate • Deep breathing • Feeling grounded	**Bodily Sensations:** • Tense muscles • Sweating • Rapid heart rate • Headache • Buzzing sensation
Workplace Symptoms: • Disengaged • Unmotivated • Distracted • Forgetful • Procrastinating	**Workplace Symptoms:** • Sharp attention • Clear decision-making • Adaptable • Sustained motivation • Enhanced problem-solving	**Workplace Symptoms:** • Impulsive choices • Agitated • Forgetful • Distracted • Tunnel vision • Avoidant • Impacted communication

Figure 1.1: Interoceptive Stress-Performance Curve (adopted from Yerkes-Dodson, 1908)

For the purposes of this chapter and for setting the stage for the discussions about stress in Chapters 2 and 3, there are a couple of points that are important to know about this widely used illustration:

1. It is an *idealized* stress-performance curve; it's an average. In actuality, the curve varies from person to person and is

influenced by circumstance, training, and physiology, so it is rarely a perfect bell shape.

2. For simple tasks, higher stress levels can help performance, such as assembly lines or repetitive manufacturing tasks, data entry, clerical work, driving (see Chapter 9 case study), flying, and marksmanship under pressure. But for complex tasks, optimal performance occurs at lower levels of stress (e.g., problem solving, creative thinking, strategic planning, collaborating with others).

This is why tuning into the body is very important: high performance on complex tasks tends to require lower stress levels than on simple tasks. As we'll explore in the book, we can harness the power of the stress-performance relationship by understanding where we fall on that curve. Interoceptive awareness enables us to identify where we are on the curve, which allows us to modulate it (dial it up or down as needed). In a sense, we can learn to manipulate our stress level, much like we do the accelerator and brake systems in a vehicle.

We are wired with a stress response system that's essential for our survival. It's what helps us react quickly, stay alert, and meet challenges effectively. When we don't know how to down-regulate the stress response or allow it to reset, it is tempting to see stress as harmful. But the problem isn't the system itself; it's only our lack of understanding of how to work with it. In reality, it's over-activation of the stress response and incomplete recovery that are the problem.

Let's return to discussing the language used for stress and how words influence our perspective, attitude, and mindset. The literature, both scientific and popular, generally discusses coping with or managing stress through social resources (talking with a trusted confidant, spending time with friends), relaxation activities (reading a book, watching a movie, taking a bath), cognitive strategies (self-talk, perspective shifting), and exercise.

As I discuss further in the book, these approaches can offer relief from stress, but they may not get us back to a baseline stress level for two main reasons. This is possible for two key reasons. One, they are less likely to give us full stress recovery unless we are intentionally tapping into our stress-recovery system, the mechanisms in our brain and body that govern this entire process. Two, while we're engaging in these activities, we may very well still be replaying or reminding ourselves (in a sense, reliving) what created the stress in the first place.

As a result, despite our efforts to "de-stress," our thoughts and mindsets about the stressful situation remain in play. If that's the case (and it so often is), it's like putting out the fire while the gas is still on. I'll talk later on about how to blend the most widely used strategies with interoceptive awareness to get to the root of the source response and recovery system, and then bring in the other approaches.

Terms like "coping with stress" or "managing stress" tend to reinforce a mindset that stress is bad and relate to being in reaction mode. They imply we're enduring something inherently unpleasant and trying to make the situation a little less difficult.

Many people have started talking about regulating stress, which I believe is more helpful than just coping with or managing it. This framing reinforces a more neutral, less narrow viewpoint of our innate response to challenges. Stress regulation is a widely used term among those who study and train in the neurophysiological aspects of stress (how the brain, nerves, and body work together to generate, use, and recover from stress). I also use this term partly out of habit, but also when I'm talking about what the brain, mind, and body are doing on their own, without help from interoceptive awareness.

While *stress regulation* is a step in the right conceptual direction, I prefer to talk about how we can *modulate* our stress response, a term we discussed in the introduction. This goes far beyond coping, managing, or even regulating stress. Modulating encompasses dialing stress up and down in our stress response. Much like adjusting a thermostat, stress modulation allows us to fine-tune our stress levels to meet the needs or demands of the moment. This helps us stay in what I like to call the "Goldilocks Zone" of stress activation, meaning we are better able to dampen or amplify stress as needed for the particular situation, keeping it *just right.*

Let's use our stress to accomplish tasks effectively, meet our goals, and end up healthier and happier in the process. This calls for doing more than coping with or managing stress. It requires that we harness this stress energy, dial it up or down to the right level, and then make sure we fully recover from it. This shift starts with changing our language around stress and learning how to modulate our stress levels.

STRESS, RESILIENCE, WELL-BEING, AND PERFORMANCE

Like common references to stress, the terms "resilience," "well-being," and "performance" are often used in ways that may be too limiting. In my work with people around the world and across many fields, I've found a number of misconceptions about these capacities and how they relate to one another. Figure 1.2 summarizes common views I come across in my work.

Common Beliefs About High Performance and Stress

High Performance	"Crushing it" at work. Producing results. Always being sure of decisions or actions. Being unemotional and always logical in decision-making. Pushing through fatigue.
↑	
Well-Being	Feeling happy. Rarely (or never) calling in sick to work. Being physically fit and free of disease. Being mentally strong. Having a 'comfortable' life.
↑	
Resilience	Bouncing back from stress, shaking things off, and getting back up when life knocks us down. Being unaffected by emotions or being able to suppress them. Needing little sleep.
↑	
Stress Management	Doing something that helps us feel calmer and more relaxed. Having some downtime. Taking a vacation.
↑	
Stress	What we feel when life throws more at us than we can handle at the time. Feeling unhappy. Feeling emotions such as anger or frustration.

Figure 1.2: Common Beliefs about high performance and stress

The conceptual understanding summarized in Figure 1.2 offers a good starting point for exploring this complex topic. But once we look more closely at the science and begin applying the research in real life, this way of thinking becomes too limited.

When scientists study something, they have to be very specific to ensure their methods and results are solid. The specialized language they use, while it can sound overly technical, actually serves a purpose. My goal is to find a way to discuss these complex phenomena without sacrificing accuracy or overwhelming or dismissing everyday definitions. I want to offer a distilled understanding of what science and experience have shown to be crucial aspects of our brain-body functioning that support sustained excellence, as outlined in Figure 1.3.

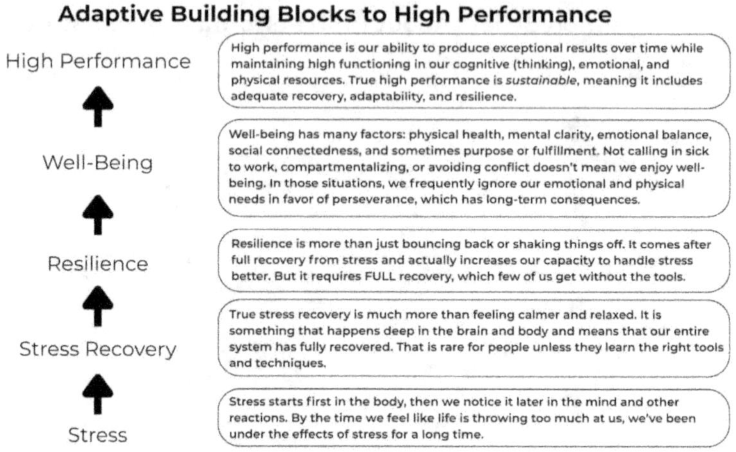

Adaptive Building Blocks to High Performance

High Performance	High performance is our ability to produce exceptional results over time while maintaining high functioning in our cognitive (thinking), emotional, and physical resources. True high performance is *sustainable*, meaning it includes adequate recovery, adaptability, and resilience.
Well-Being	Well-being has many factors: physical health, mental clarity, emotional balance, social connectedness, and sometimes purpose or fulfillment. Not calling in sick to work, compartmentalizing, or avoiding conflict doesn't mean we enjoy well-being. In those situations, we frequently ignore our emotional and physical needs in favor of perseverance, which has long-term consequences.
Resilience	Resilience is more than just bouncing back or shaking things off. It comes after full recovery from stress and actually increases our capacity to handle stress better. But it requires FULL recovery, which few of us get without the tools.
Stress Recovery	True stress recovery is much more than feeling calmer and relaxed. It is something that happens deep in the brain and body and means that our entire system has fully recovered. That is rare for people unless they learn the right tools and techniques.
Stress	Stress starts first in the body, then we notice it later in the mind and other reactions. By the time we feel like life is throwing too much at us, we've been under the effects of stress for a long time.

Figure 1.3: Adaptive building blocks for high performance

These brief definitions are based on science and research, and on my own preferences for clarity, which come from studying these topics, practicing these techniques, getting certified in a number of related human-performance tools, and teaching these topics and techniques for almost 20 years.

You'll see these terms, along with others like "autonomic nervous system," "neurophysiological regulation," "psychological regulation," and "interoceptive awareness," throughout the book. For now, let's turn to what underpins well-being and high performance: resilience.

Resilience is our ability to stay regulated and responsive when challenged. Psychiatrist Dan Siegel speaks about the *window of tolerance* to describe the zone in which our nervous system can stay flexible and integrated, thereby increasing our capacity to face challenges (Siegel, 2012). In this book, I build on that idea by focusing on how interoceptive awareness helps us modulate stress arousal, not simply tolerate more stress, so we can meet the demands of the moment with clarity and resilience.

So, resilience is much more than bouncing back, and it is not a single, catch-all capacity like mental toughness or a calm exterior under pressure. I find that resilience is often mistaken for grit or stoicism, which is our ability to stay composed under pressure and push through no matter what.

In reality, resilience is not about suppression or endurance, nor is it a one-dimensional strength. It is expressed through interconnected domains of functioning (physical, psychological, cognitive, and social) that continually influence one another (see Figure 1.4) and rest entirely on the brain–body systems that regulate stress and recovery. Importantly, when resilience is compromised in one domain, the effects tend to spill over and degrade resilience in other domains.

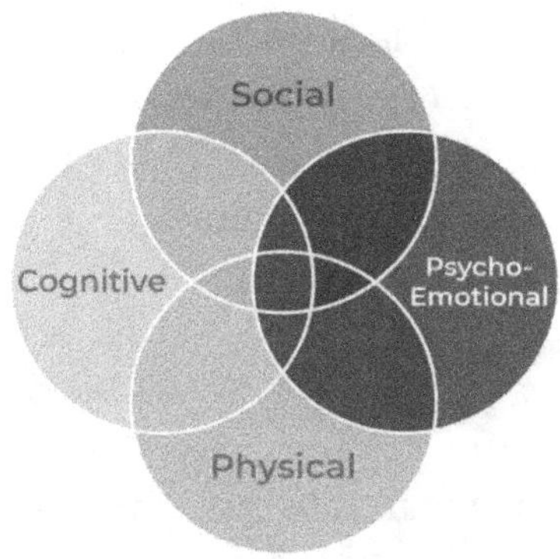

Figure 1.4 The main domains of resilience

Physical resilience means we enjoy efficient stress recovery in the body, such as endurance, immune function, and healing. A key aspect of **psychological/emotional (psych-emotional) resilience** is our ability to experience and regulate the full range of emotions without being overwhelmed, as well as maintain emotional stability and adaptability, even in stressful circumstances. **Cognitive resilience** shows up as, for example, sustained focus, flexibility in our thinking and perspective-taking, and clear decision-making under pressure. Last but not least, when we have high **social resilience,** we're able to maintain relationships (even through high-stress times) that are grounded in empathy, compassion, and fairness. We are able to adjust to another person's needs as circumstances change, and our relationships foster safety, trust, and co-regulation (helping each other stay steady in tough times).

Many models add further dimensions to resilience (such as spiritual, moral, or cultural), recognizing that meaning, purpose, and belonging can help us cope with challenges. My focus here, however, is on the four primary domains shown above because they are most immediately shaped by how well we regulate stress (how effectively the body and mind can activate, adapt, and return to balance).

Our level of resilience in one domain tends to affect the others. If we're low in physical resilience, we often see lower resilience in our emotional realm, for example. When we improve in one domain, we tend to lift the level of the others up as well. I find this useful to discuss with my clients and workshop participants because it's easy to be unaware of how our resilience is faring if we don't see the full picture across multiple domains.

> Resilience is a state, not a trait. It shows up (and is impacted by) multiple domains of our lives, which in turn affects other domains. We are born with different capacities for resilience, but we can increase capacity according to how well or how fully we recover from stress.

A FOUNDATION OF RESILIENCE: OUR NERVOUS SYSTEM

When we get all the way down to the basics of resilience, we're dealing with the biological system or systems that generate the stress response and help us recover from it.

The autonomic nervous system (ANS) provides the foundation for resilience by regulating how we mobilize energy, recover from stress, and return to a steady state. Without ANS flexibility, psychological resilience has little ground to stand on. The ANS is the part of our nervous system that controls our automatic life-sustaining functions, such as heart rate, breathing, and digestion (among others). You might remember from a long-ago biology class that the sympathetic branch (SNS) of the ANS is like the accelerator, or gas pedal. It revs us up (fight-or-flight) to have the energy to deal with a challenge or threat. A more technical description of this is "stress activation."

Conversely, the parasympathetic branch (PNS) is like the brake pedal; it slows the body down so that we can rest and recover. These two branches are in a continuous metaphorical dance, with one leading and then the other. Both branches are always "on," but one will be more influential than the other depending on what the brain perceives is needed. Stress resilience depends on how well the ANS can shift back and forth between activation and recovery. Tracking your heart rate variability, or HRV, is one of the easiest ways to get a sense of the state of balance between these two branches—how flexibly our ANS balances the activity of the SNS and the PNS.

When I talk in the book about neurophysiological (self) regulation, I'm referring to tapping into the ANS through practices and techniques to directly affect these two branches of the ANS. I will refer to this as "bottom-up stress regulation."

Very often in articles and books, stress regulation is discussed only in terms of psychological regulation, which I refer to as "top-down stress regulation." Top-down regulation techniques and strategies rely on our conscious minds to try to control the ANS, often referred to as cognitive strategies. They include approaches like reframing or reappraising a situation, positive self-talk, looking for possible benefits in a difficult situation, and so forth.

Based on my background in psychotherapy and my years of coaching and training people to improve resilience and performance under stress, I have found that the most effective and sustainable way to improve resilience and enhance performance under stress is to blend neurophysiological (bottom-up) approaches with psychological (top-down) regulation techniques. Figure 1.5 illustrates the approach I consider most effective for moving toward sustained high performance.

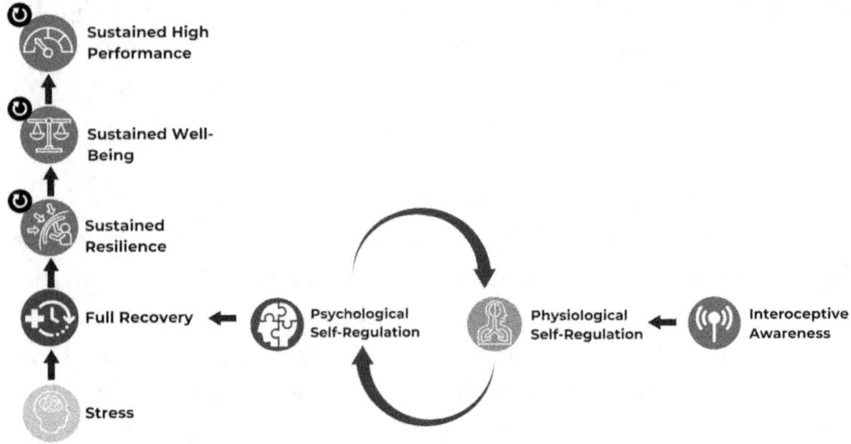

Figure 1.5: The path from stress to sustained high performance

Two powerful capacity-building approaches are mindfulness practices and Somatic Experiencing (SE). Both are important to interoceptive awareness. Let's take a very quick look at these approaches.

MINDFULNESS AND SOMATIC EXPERIENCING (SE) IN A NUTSHELL

Mindfulness has become a mainstream topic over the past decade, and the price of its popularity has been the watering down or distortion of the tradition. Mindfulness is not the same thing as simply paying attention to what we say or how we say it, and it is not about relaxing. Mindfulness is about focused attention, awareness, and, very importantly, allowing for all experiences (meaning we are aware of experiences without being controlled or jerked around by them). A foundational element of mindfulness practice is noticing sensations in the body, which is the act of consciously engaging in interoception. In mindfulness practice, there's no cognitive interpretation of sensation; instead, it's simply an awareness of sensation as a building block of mindful awareness and focused attention.

While mindfulness practices include noticing bodily sensations (e.g., body scan, sensing the breath, sensing the activities of walking), the aim is not to build interoceptive awareness. Mindfulness uses noticing as an opportunity to build a capacity of non-judgment and allow for all experiences. It is important to note that practicing mindfulness is best done by working with a qualified teacher. Depending on the level of dysregulation in the ANS (from intense chronic stress or trauma, for example), great care needs to be taken before jumping in.

Somatic Experiencing (SE) is a body-based trauma-resolution approach that can be hugely instrumental in helping us connect with sensations, weak and strong, and learn to regulate them by allowing the body's wisdom to collaborate with our cognitive capacities. It is a powerful approach to neurophysiological management of stress that arises when working through traumatic events and experiences, and it is a fabulous way to simply learn to regulate the ANS, whether you have experienced trauma or not.

As mentioned in the introduction, and something I'll discuss more in Chapter 3, our modern lifestyle offers ample opportunity for our attention to be pulled away from our bodies, causing the volume to be turned way down so that we can no longer hear information that influences just about every aspect of our functioning.

As a coach and trainer, I see so many people negatively impacted by this body silence. The challenge is that we're so conditioned to believe that all change happens in the mind, and often even the most motivated clients struggle to accept that the body must be part of the change process. There are a number of reasons for this (feeling too pressed for time, being conditioned to rely too much on mental effort, having emotional or physical trauma), so that it makes tuning into the body unfamiliar or, perhaps, uncomfortable at first. Figure 1.6 highlights some of the most common reasons people have shared with me over the years for feeling unsure about tuning into their bodies.

What Holds Us Back From Tuning In To Our Bodies

Figure 1.6: Common reasons to avoid pausing and tuning into the body

Eventually, they feel the difference and see enormous changes that come from rebuilding their sensitivity to bodily signals and learning how to interpret and use that information. Interoceptive awareness is often transformational and life-changing once clients *feel* the effects of tuning in and regulating stress and then seeing the potential of this newfound (or renewed) powerhouse of well-being and performance. *Feeling, rather than seeing, is believing!*

Okay, let's dig into defining stress and explore how we can make it work for us.

Chapter Two

CATCHING STRESS IN THE ACT

"There cannot be a stressful crisis next week. My schedule is already full."
—Henry Kissinger

KEY TAKEAWAYS:

- Stress is a normal part of our lives. We need it to be resilient.
- Most of us don't realize how much stress we're holding onto.
- We can learn to make stress work for us if we catch it early and modulate it.
- High interoceptive awareness is critical for noticing stress as it first shows up and modulating it.

I love talking about stress. I usually get a chuckle or a smile when I say that at the beginning of workshops, but it's true. I love this topic because it's something we all experience all the time, whether we allow it into our schedules or not (a reference to Mr. Kissinger!). It is a natural part of life, and while most people assume the best they can do is manage it, in reality, it can be modulated, dialed up or down, through our own efforts. Our typical daily stress levels keep our nervous system overly activated for optimal performance. Yet there are times when it is too low to perform at our best.

This chapter deals mostly with understanding stress arousal that exceeds our capacity to think clearly, making decisions that align with our goals and values, maintaining connection with others, listening to understand rather than respond, and avoiding feeling drained at the end of the day. So, I will focus on stress regulation (dialing it down) in this chapter.

Stress regulation is how we bring the body and mind back into balance after stress has been triggered. Stress modulation is how we influence stress in real time, dialing it up or down to stay within our optimal zone for learning, communication, connection, well-being, and high performance.

I use different metaphors to describe how our stress system works. Sometimes I describe stress as the brain/body system's way of "revving our engines" to give us the fuel to respond to changing driving conditions. The point of this chapter is to introduce the reality that we have an innate ability to manipulate the accelerator and brake systems to arrive at our destination without undue wear and tear on the engine.

Stress modulation offers huge potential for meeting your goals and becoming the person you want to be. As a coach and a trainer/facilitator, I urge clients to catch stress in the act. The sooner we recognize our signature signs of stress, and the more we practice regulating them, the more we make stress our ally.

So, I'll ask you now the same question I ask all coaching clients and workshop participants at some point: How do you *first* know that you're stressed? What are the signs? Take a moment now to think about that and jot down what first comes to mind. Usually, one or two people will list signs like "my heart beats faster," "my jaw gets tight," or "my breathing gets faster and moves higher into the chest." List those under "immediate."

For signs such as headaches, fidgetiness, restlessness, upset stomach, or difficulty concentrating, I note them under "short-term," meaning the symptoms might appear minutes to hours after the stress response.

Often, the longest list falls under the medium-term signs (when our stress level is too high for days or weeks) and includes sleep issues, teeth grinding, mood swings, overindulging in comfort foods or alcohol, or a number of other indicators that show we're out of balance.

Then come the long-term effects that might indicate months to years of unregulated chronic stress, such as compromised immunity (ranging from more frequent colds to serious illnesses), burnout, depression (which may be physical exhaustion rather than clinical depression, but those can look and feel the same), weight gain or loss, memory issues or foggy thinking, digestive disorders, and hair loss. Figure 2.1 below provides some indicators of immediate, medium-term, and chronic stress.

Immediate Symptoms	**Medium** Symptoms	**Chronic** Symptoms
Clenched Fists Rapid or Slowed Heart Rate Perspiration Achy Muscles Headache Clenched Jaw	Trouble Focusing Trouble Sleeping Upset Stomach	Losing Hair Insomnia Depression Panic Attacks Damaged Relationships Avoidant

Figure 2.1: Examples of immediate, medium-term, and longer term signs of stress

After asking many thousands of people over the past 20 years the basic question, "How do you first know you're stressed?" I have come to a few conclusions:

1. A lot of us have chronic stress that is unrecognized and therefore unmanaged.
2. We are either not aware of immediate, short-term, and even medium-term signs of stress, or we deliberately ignore them and push on.
3. We all have two pathways for working with our stress response: a fast one through the body and a slow one through the mind. Both work, but starting with the body helps quiet the biological stress response before we engage the thinking brain, so our self-talk is more effective, and perspective shifts are more stable.

FAST VS. SLOW PATHWAYS TO STRESS REGULATION

It surprises most people to learn that stress first shows up in the body (i.e., that is where we can first become aware of it), and catching it there is the fastest path to regulating it. Borrowing another metaphor to explain this complex system, think of the brain as a smoke alarm: when it senses a challenge or threat, it automatically signals the body (heart, lungs, muscles, etc.). This happens within milliseconds, and if we're tuned in, we *could* quickly notice (very soon after the stress response is launched) indications like increased heart rate, warmth (our body temperature rising), faster and shallower breathing, jaw tightening, and so on.

At this point, we can take action to down-regulate the stress to a helpful level. We can turn our attention to sensations of our bodies in contact with a physical surface (chair, floor, etc.) and allow the jaw to slacken or the shoulders to fall back onto the shoulder blades, which assists the brain-body system in initiating the regulation process. This body-based (bottom-up) approach to stress regulation has an immediate and direct impact on the neurophysiological system, likely allowing the ANS to begin returning to greater balance.

People with high interoceptive awareness skills can notice stress in the body within 10 or 15 seconds, though most people don't realize they are stressed until minutes after the initial stress activation. Some might not be conscious of their stress for days, weeks, or months, all while their stress level, or allostatic load, is very likely inching up.

If we can't catch the initial signals in the body, stress will eventually show up in the mind (thoughts, moods, perspectives, biases) or in our behaviors, actions, tone of voice, choice of words, and so on. At this point, we still have the option of trying to start the regulation process in the body.

Most people have not learned or developed habits for bottom-up regulation approaches and instead rely on top-down techniques, such as positive self-talk, shifting perspective, or reframing the situation, as well as social connection (note: socializing with people who help us feel comfortable and safe is a helpful skill), exercise, and distraction or self-soothing behaviors, such as playing a video game, watching a show or movie, drinking alcohol, or eating comfort food.

It's more efficient to catch stress as soon as it shows up in the body, rather than relying on the other approaches. By the time our mind gets involved, trying to reframe the situation or organize around other standard stress-management approaches, we are already well into the stress cascade. This is why I find it more effective to first go directly to the system, the fast path that mobilizes the stress energy, and then bring other approaches into the process.

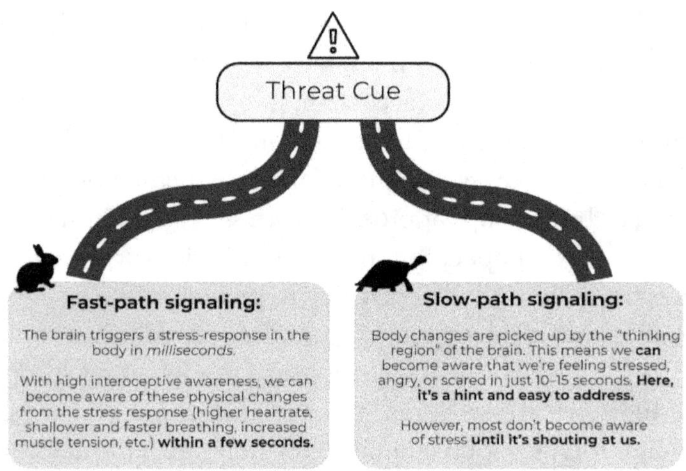

Figure 2.2: Fast vs. slow stress-awareness pathways

Our ANS is trying to bring us back into balance all the time, but it's fighting an uphill battle when our minds can't reframe the situation effectively or quickly enough. If we can't get to the gym to work off some of the stress energy (or if we replay the source of the stress in our minds while exercising), if our friend is not available, if we can't take a bath, or read a book, where does that leave us? Typically, by this point, stress is on its merry way, and it can become harder and harder to tackle.

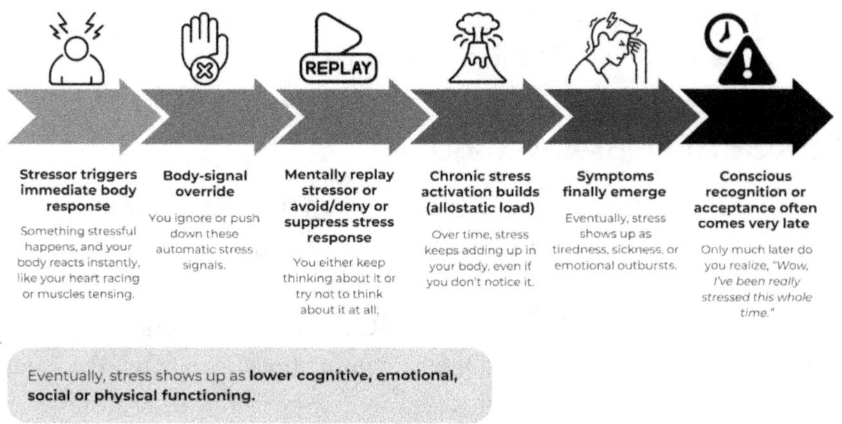

Figure 2.3: Downsides to delayed stress-modulation

This is why I am so invested in teaching interoceptive awareness. There is no downside, in my experience, to catching the stress response early, and no negative results from directly assisting the brain-body system in returning to balance. The only challenge is that most of us have not been taught to stay attuned to our bodies and their signals. In fact, most of us are encouraged by society to ignore all signs of stress, even those that seep into our minds.

So, instead of minutes, it may take weeks (or months) of accumulated stress before we realize we are stressed. Since physical signs of stress show up within milliseconds in the body, catching it there offers the biggest bang for the buck. If we wait until our mind catches up to make sense of the stress or wait until later to get to the gym or running trail, stress has been hard at work, impacting us in ways we often don't realize.

A key goal of my coaching and training is to help people learn to catch stress signals early, so they are better able to modulate their stress levels (to allow it to work for, not against, them). Catching stress early is the most efficient way to decide if it's at the right level and then using appropriate techniques to dial it up or down as needed.

The following sections provide some real-life examples of people

I've worked with in group settings or individually who suffered due to a lack of awareness of their stress levels.

SERGEANT BACA: 0-60

I had the huge honor of working with our U.S. military for over a decade as a resilience subject-matter expert. In addition to working with active-duty Army and Marines during that time, I facilitated hundreds of sessions for the Yellow Ribbon Reintegration Program (YRRP), a Department of Defense program supporting the well-being of National Guard and Reserve members and their families.

> The YRRP supports National Guard and Reserve service members and their families before, during, and after deployment by promoting readiness, connection, and resilience. Its events are designed to provide information, resources, and support that ease transitions, strengthen relationships, and foster successful reintegration into civilian and family life.

During one weekend-long event, I was facilitating sessions on anger management and the emotional cycles of deployment with a group of fifty military police who had recently returned from a particularly intense and psychologically challenging deployment to Guantanamo Bay in the early years of detainee-related security missions.

Within seconds of asking my standard question, "How do you *first* know that you're stressed?"

Sergeant Baca raised his hand and said, "When I want to throw a chair at somebody." I looked at him silently for a few seconds, seeing if he wanted to add anything. The expression on my face may have told him I thought he was pulling my leg because he added, "Really, that's how I first know I'm stressed!"

A number of his buddies chimed in, saying, "Yes, ma'am, that's true."

I asked, "Okay, so you go from 0 to 60 before you notice that you're feeling stressed?" to which he nodded his head and said, "Yes, ma'am."

Over the past 20-plus years of working with people in many different professions from more than 25 countries and subcultures, I find that few are aware of how stress shows up until it has been acting on them for some time. Thankfully, most don't get to the point of wanting to pick up furniture and throw it. But many carry around stress for a long time and don't even know it until their health takes a negative turn: they develop insomnia, damage relationships, are reprimanded at work, or experience a host of other unpleasant outcomes.

It's like carrying around a backpack every day with rocks being added to it moment by moment. During sleep (if it's sufficient and high-quality), we unload some of the rocks, but we may still wake up with a *stress backpack* that hasn't emptied (see Figure 2.4). While our load may not be as heavy as Sergeant Baca's and our first indication of feeling stressed isn't wanting to throw a chair, our stress backpack is often heavier than most of us realize. The reason is that we're simply not familiar with what full recovery feels like.

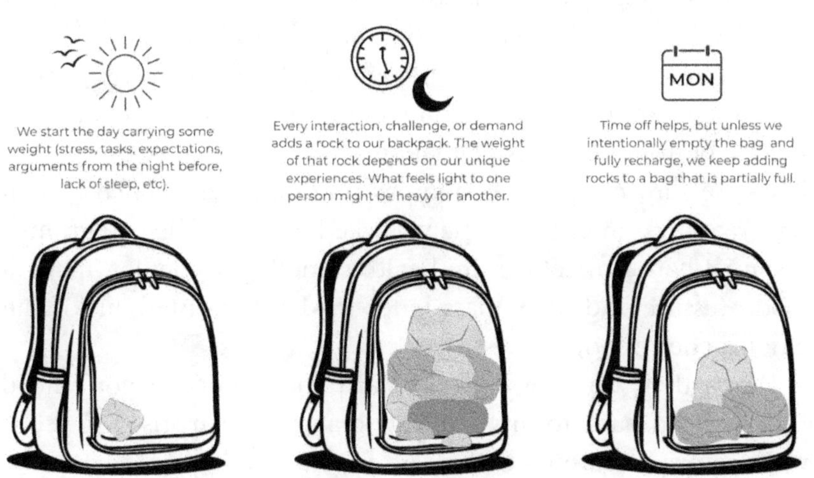

Figure 2.4: Carrying our stress backpacks

BILL: FLYING BLIND

The majority of people I work with are not like Sergeant Baca. They don't go from zero to 60 without realizing they are stressed. Bill is a good example of many of my clients.

A few years ago, I conducted monthly trainings for different cohorts of U.S. Department of Defense employees heading to Afghanistan as part of the Expeditionary Civilian workforce. These groups were tasked with assisting the Afghans to build institutional capacity in areas such as IT, engineering, construction, human resources, finance management, logistics, and contracting, among others. To prepare them for their mission, each cohort went through an intense two-week pre-deployment course, during which they trained for about 12 hours a day, seven days a week. They had almost no privacy and very little downtime.

As I always do in sessions on resilience, I asked the group for examples of their stressors. Most of the group freely offered some, but one guy, Bill, in the back of the room, leaned back on his chair and said, "Ma'am, I just don't get stressed."

I pressed him a bit. "Really? Never stressed?"

"No, ma'am," he responded.

"Wow," I said, "I can't imagine what that would be like!"

As time marched on with this group, I taught classes and also spent a two-week training period supporting those who wanted to practice bottom-up stress-regulation techniques before getting their blood pressure checked. A number of them were concerned that their readings might get them kicked out of the program, as personnel had to meet certain health standards to deploy, including blood pressure and body mass index (BMI). Bill opted out of these extra practice opportunities.

When their training and medical period ended, I got onto the plane to head back to my home state and was surprised to see Bill on the jetway, assuming he was on his way to Afghanistan with his cohort. He told me that he was sent home for high BMI (which made him ineligible for deployment). We spoke for a few minutes about the training and the people in his class. "Man, I hated those people!" he went on to say. "I wanted to strangle every single one of them! They drove me crazy!"

So much for never getting stressed. Did he not realize that he was experiencing stress during these two weeks of living and training in close quarters with virtual strangers in preparation to head to a war zone for a year? Or was he just not able to admit it? I'll never know, but there are many people like him who are either completely unaware of what stress looks and feels like or, for some reason, won't admit it. A lot of people avoid admitting they feel stressed, as if acknowledging it means they're not strong enough. But stress isn't a flaw in character or a sign of weakness. Experiencing stress is a feature of being human, and being honest with ourselves about our stress triggers and stress signals offers a powerful advantage.

DANIELLE: DASHBOARD DARK

Nowadays, most of my clients are much more like Danielle, a high-potential at a tech company headquartered in Palo Alto, California. Danielle seemed to be doing great and was on her way up in the company. As an engineering team lead, she had consistently been a high performer since joining the organization, proving herself to be dependable, technically capable, and unflappable even in chaos. She was up for a promotion, and as part of her development and transition plan, her higher-ups brought me in as a coach to support her leadership skills, focusing on emotional intelligence and communication. Danielle felt more than ready for the next level and beyond. She told me that she had always been able to push through, was mentally tough, and always got the task done, no matter what. She was proud of her record, rightfully so, and had been consistently recognized in both performance reviews and pay.

There was no reason to believe that her performance trend would not continue indefinitely. And, if performance metrics were the only important indicator, that would have been a reasonable assumption. We all have different levels of stress tolerance. This resilience is based on biological, psychological, and environmental factors, and I recognized that Danielle might be one of those very rare people who have that mix of factors that make her extremely resilient, able to experience intense stress without suffering short- or long-term negative effects.

During our initial coaching conversations, however, it became clearer that stress had been building. She acknowledged signs of *something* being off from time to time but disregarded them, unaware of their importance. Like most people I work with, she figured whatever was going on in terms of stress would go away as soon as the current project was completed: a chronically tight jaw; increased heart rate during tough conversations; faster, more shallow breathing before meetings; periodic difficulty prioritizing; less tolerance for uncertainty; more difficulty reframing a difficult event or situation; intermittent digestion troubles; difficulty falling asleep; headaches that seemed to come on suddenly.

There was more. Danielle led a team of fifteen people who were meeting their targets, so she assumed all was well. However, results from a performance review indicated that she felt a little different in the past six months or so. Write-in comments indicated that she was less patient with their questions or requests, showing signs of irritation when they didn't follow her point or didn't understand quickly enough. Some said she seemed to need more control and was becoming more rigid in her thinking and requests. Others even said her decision-making style felt different, either hesitating to make decisions or making them hastily.

Despite the signs, though, nobody seemed to think that she was struggling with anything serious. They chalked it up to long work hours and tight deadlines, saying it was to be expected given the demands of their projects. As is the case with many of my clients, these signs of stress were considered acceptable. She still wasn't concerned.

After a couple of coaching sessions, Danielle started to acknowledge that chronic stress was taking a bite out of her. She revealed that her personal relationships had been suffering for some time, her sleep was terrible, and that, at 35 years of age, she was told she should consider taking blood pressure medication. She also told me that although she had always been on the lean side and was a generally very happy person, she had started to gain belly fat and feel down. All of these were likely indications of dysregulated chronic stress.

Leadership had specifically asked me to help Danielle improve her leadership skills around emotional intelligence and communication. Before we started working on these, however, we needed to build her capacity to recognize bodily stress and modulate it.

Danielle was in a chronically heightened stress state, which limited her access to foundational capacities for emotional intelligence and good communication: empathy, impulse control, perspective taking, and active listening. I explained to leadership that we couldn't build advanced capabilities on a faulty (stress-dysregulated) foundation.

Figure 2.4: Resilience energizes well-being and performance

INTEROCEPTIVE AWARENESS: INTERNAL SAFETY NET AND GUIDANCE SYSTEM

Danielle's lack of awareness or concern isn't surprising or rare. Most of us do not grow up encouraged to pause and notice what we are experiencing. This is true for big experiences and small ones.

Despite the pace of our lives and how easy it is to get pulled from one thing to the next, we are not encouraged to stop and pay attention to our bodies, to sensations. And yet, these sensations remain at the core of our functioning.

We learn our mother language and perhaps one or two (or several) more as we move through life. These are crucial to meeting our needs, though we often don't think of language in this way. To me, it is just as important to learn to speak the language between the body and the brain that keeps us alive and functioning well: interoception. Sensations, like butterflies in the stomach or a quickened heart rate, are your vocabulary; interoceptive awareness is your fluency.

However, most of us don't learn that these bodily signals are continuously sent to the brain, allowing the body to communicate in the only possible way whether we are in or out of balance. If we learned growing up how interoception influences nearly every human function, including emotion regulation, decision-making, focus, physical health, resilience, and social connection, we just might pay closer attention and try to learn how to speak this language, helping the brain-body out in its ongoing efforts to keep us alive and to thrive.

We do our best in our very busy lives, handling the daily challenges, unaware that this conversation is happening between the body and the brain to keep us functioning well. We don't realize that when this language gets distorted by chronic stress, the messaging gets muffled or misinterpreted, making it harder for our system to stay in balance.

As a result, we tend to treat our brains and bodies like a car we drive at high speeds, accelerating into and around the corners, then slamming the brakes as we approach the end of the trip. We tend to ignore scheduled maintenance that addresses the core elements of the system that make the car run and ignore signs that the car needs attention, like low oil pressure, poor tire alignment, flickering dashboard lights, and so on. When it comes to our brains and bodies, it's very common for us to realize our system is wearing down only after something serious happens. Ironically, many of us maintain our cars better than we do our own physical and mental systems.

Without regular and full reregulation from a nonstop stress load, we will reach a breaking point, which can show up in many different ways. We might first see issues with our information processing, memory, decision-making capacity, or cognitive flexibility. Or we might notice that we're less adaptable during times of uncertainty and change. We might be more susceptible to issues with our physical health or a number of other indications that our system needs more than a tune-up; it's calling for an overhaul.

I do not want anyone to run into problems because they have willfully ignored their need for stress regulation to save time, or because they didn't know to look for signs of stress and how to down-regulate it.

I chose the stories in this book to illustrate the thousands of people I have worked with because most people fall into one of the three categories:

1. I may have worked with more people like Sergeant Baca than I realized (few will admit their first sign of stress is wanting to throw a piece of furniture at someone).
2. I have worked with people like Bill who are either completely unaware of what a stress response feels like or won't admit it.
3. Many of my clients are like Danielle, high-performing people who recognize that they are stressed but are convinced they can't afford the time to down-regulate it, and they can deal with it when they take a vacation or retire.

It is common to feel energized by a challenge or risky undertaking. This level of stress arousal is pleasant and can help us focus and be productive. This energizing, exciting level of stress is what drives many high performers. That's great, until it's not. Most people haven't been taught how to know when helpful stress turns harmful (more on helpful versus unhelpful stress in Chapter 3). Many thrive on the thrill of professional challenges only to be surprised after decades of this pace to develop diabetes, hypertension, vascular cognitive impairment, or other potential disorders and diseases that are either directly linked to unregulated chronic stress or strongly exacerbated by it.

My experience working with high-performing individuals and teams in demanding contexts tells me that few people recognize the impact of unregulated chronic stress on cognitive capacities, mood, weight changes, and other performance and well-being factors. Many simply do not want to believe that stress is getting the better of them. Because of a lack of awareness, people just keep chugging along, putting more and more "rocks into their backpacks" without really feeling the extra weight. They have become accustomed to lugging around a heavy pack.

My goal is to help everyone, from the super high-performer to the person who is just trying to get through daily challenges. My hope is to help every person interested in being healthier, happier, in better relationships, and performing better understand the value of habitually assessing the weight of their backpacks so that they can unload it, boulder by boulder. I want people to realize that by doing this, they are increasing the capacity of their stress backpack, which is about as close to a superpower as we'll ever get.

Interoceptive awareness is key to that superpower. If you allow me to shift metaphors once again, building interoceptive awareness is like running a dynamic brain-body system-monitoring program that also makes real-time adjustments based on stress levels and what is needed for optimal performance. The more we engage interoceptive awareness, the more we enhance our ability to down-regulate, fully recover from stress, and use our full range of intelligence. This supports high performance and well-being, even under difficult conditions and when the stakes are high.

Chapter Three

BUILDING A PORTABLE STRESS-MODULATION TOOLKIT

"We are what we repeatedly do. Excellence, then, is not an act but a habit."
—*Will Durant*, summarizing Aristotle in
The Story of Philosophy (1926)

KEY TAKEAWAYS:

- Stress is energy mobilized so we can respond to a demand for change.
- Our current-day stress is more chronic and harder to recover from than that of past generations.
- Interoceptive awareness + neurophysiological regulation + psychological regulation = more sustainable high performance and well-being.
- When we dial up or down our stress level, we move from regulating stress to modulating it.

After dipping our toes in the water and getting familiar with the surface of how stress shows up, I now want to wade in a little deeper to explore what's happening beneath those indicators of stress, explore why we seem to have more stress now than past generations, and offer ideas on how to build a stress-modulation toolkit.

As mentioned in Chapter 1, stress is the brain and body's way of mobilizing energy to meet a demand for change, such as in response to a real or perceived challenge or threat. Stress begins as a physical surge in the body, triggered by the brain. After that, it can show in our thoughts, thought patterns, moods, etc. I again emphasize this point from Chapter 2 because people tend to first become aware of stress in the mind (worry, racing thoughts, etc.), so they assume that's where it starts. As mentioned previously, if we wait to address stress once it shows up in our thoughts and moods, we are behind the curve and have to put in more effort to dial back our stress to a more productive level.

Science shows us that stress is a brain-body event, and the first recognizable response is physical. Mental events (negative thoughts, difficult memories, self-criticism, catastrophizing, fear of failure, etc.) can trigger a stress response, but the response to that internal event will first appear in the body. In this case, the mental event becomes the stress trigger; the brain reacts and sends the stress signals to the body, which manifest like any other stress response (tense muscles, stomach contractions, increased heart rate, and so on).

The good news is that we have more control over this stress cascade of changes than most realize. As mentioned in Chapter 2, our ability to effectively down-regulate stress is strongest if we notice these changes soon after they are generated, i.e., in our bodies. Part of this learning process is to pay attention to how it typically shows up for us. Then, we can employ techniques to modulate it in the body, which makes it so much easier to then benefit from cognitive, social, and passive strategies.

Let's talk more about how it shows up in the body. While all bodies experience similar changes, we may notice some more easily than others. Our heart rate increases, breathing becomes faster and shallower, mouths become drier (salivary glands slow down), muscles tense up, skin conductance changes (perhaps sweat on palms or soles of feet, skin pallor changes, etc.), pupils dilate, and gut sensations change (tightness or fluttering in the stomach, perhaps nausea), as prime examples. I have asked thousands of people from all professions about *any* physical signs of stress they notice, and I get the gamut of responses. We are all attuned to some signs more than others.

In a typical, healthy brain-body system, in every moment (even when we are sitting still, thinking about little, doing little, or even meditating), the internal system that governs our stress response and recovery, the ANS, is cycling between getting ready for action and resting and restoring.

When we inhale, our sympathetic nervous system, which prepares us for action, causes our heart rate to go up; this is natural stress activation, or fight-or-flight. When we exhale, the parasympathetic branch of the ANS, which helps us recover, causes our heart rate to go down, often called "rest and digest."

All this to say that stress and recovery are naturally occurring, and our ANS constantly adjusts our physiology to match what our environment demands, mobilizing stress energy (activation) when we need energy and focus and promoting rest and recovery (restoration) when the demand has passed.

As discussed earlier in the book, our brain-body system is designed to fully recover from a stress response and become more resilient. When we support *neurophysiological recovery* through practices that actually shift our nervous system state, we can build resilience and gradually expand our capacity to handle future stressors.

DO WE HAVE MORE STRESS THAN PAST GENERATIONS?

Stress is talked about more and more in our homes, schools, places of work, and the press. But is it because we are more aware of stress, or do we actually have more stress than people in past generations did? The answer is twofold.

Generally speaking, we are talking about it more openly and with greater scientific understanding. So, yes, we do seem to be more conscious of stress and the negative effects of having chronically high levels. But research across psychology, neuroscience, sociology, and public health also indicates that the stress we experience today is more persistent and biologically taxing than that of earlier generations (Gluckman and Hanson 2006; Lieberman 2013; McEwen and Wingfield 2003; Sapolsky 2004).

In our post-industrial, middle-to-high-income societies, research indicates that not only do we have more stress, but the kind of stress we experience now (versus in past generations) is more difficult to down-regulate.

PAST VERSUS CURRENT-DAY STRESSORS

Over the last 200 years, past generations lived through more physical, time-bound, and concrete conditions than we do today. During that time, much of the stress was related to subsistence activities, such as farming, hunting, factory work, mining, and manual labor. Stressors were physically intense but followed a rhythm, were more concrete and predictable, and relied on social interdependence, shared responsibilities, and clear social roles.

What about today? If I were to ask you to make a list of what is creating stress for you (in fact, let's do that), you would likely have triggers that fall into one or more of the following types:

- Lifestyle demands (overwork, burnout, productivity pressure, constant electronic notifications and the urge to respond immediately, sleep disruption)

- Work demands (workload, time pressure, role ambiguity, job insecurity, lack of control or autonomy, toxic bosses, difficult team members)
- Financial demands (debt, income instability, healthcare costs, global economic uncertainty)
- Relationship demands (day-to-day conflicts at home or work, child or parental caregiving, grief over breakups, divorce, death of loved ones, including pets)
- Social fears (public speaking, performance reviews, judgment from others, rejection, exclusion)
- Global uncertainty and sociopolitics (political polarization, global conflict and terrorism, social fragmentation, rapid cultural change, lingering pandemic-related stress)
- Environmental & Structural Stressors (fear and displacement from climate change, unsafe neighborhoods, crowding and lack of green space, noise pollution)

Add to that the anxiety of information overload, social isolation, identity stress, concerns over health and healthcare access, and let's add a dollop of social media impact on top. The list goes on. Such symbolic and ambiguous stressors are, as studies suggest, more toxic than the physical stress experienced in past generations.

For the vast majority of humans in post-industrialized societies, today's stressors don't come from life-or-death situations, nor from the physical demands of working the farm, hunting for dinner, getting water from the well, or working in the coal mines (although they are still part of life for some). Much of our stress stems from emotions, and research shows that the body and brain respond in similar ways to perceived threats (many rooted in emotions, such as psychosocial or existential challenges) as they do physical threats (Barrett 2017; Damasio 1994; Dickerson and Kemeny 2004).

Many of my clients deny they have stressors rooted in emotions, thinking for some reason that they are never affected by emotions. However, decades of research from the fields of neuroscience, psychology, and behavioral economics tell us that we are emotional beings and that thinking and emotions constantly interact.

Even people who claim they are "not emotional" experience emotions. I've had more than one workshop participant or coaching client try to convince me that they are not emotional, that their decisions are never based on, or influenced by, emotions. People who appear not to experience emotions are almost never emotionless; they typically have difficulty noticing, accessing, or expressing emotions. The emotions are there; the awareness is not. Emotion is not optional. It is a core operating system of the human brain-body network. Humans are emotional beings, and part of managing our stress involves being aware of our emotional responses and how emotions impact our perceptions and choices.

WHY DOES STRESS SEEM TO BE WORSE NOW?

If stress is stress, even if we have different stressors than our forebearers, why does it seem like we have more stress these days? Interestingly, humans aren't optimized for the types of stressors we're facing, and certainly not for so many coming on top of one another. As far as our brain-body system is concerned, we are supposed to be running from large animals or fighting the neighboring tribe, not running up against a project deadline or fighting to get into the lane on a crowded Los Angeles freeway. We are not wired for the psychological stressors that we face all day long.

Robert Sapolsky, a Stanford professor in the departments of biology, neurology and neurological sciences, and neurosurgery, explores the effects of long-term psychological stress in *Why Zebras Don't Get Ulcers*. He, and many others, discuss how humans have sources of stress that wild animals don't. Human systems are optimized for immediate, life-threatening dangers, not for chronic overload from the types of pressures we experience.

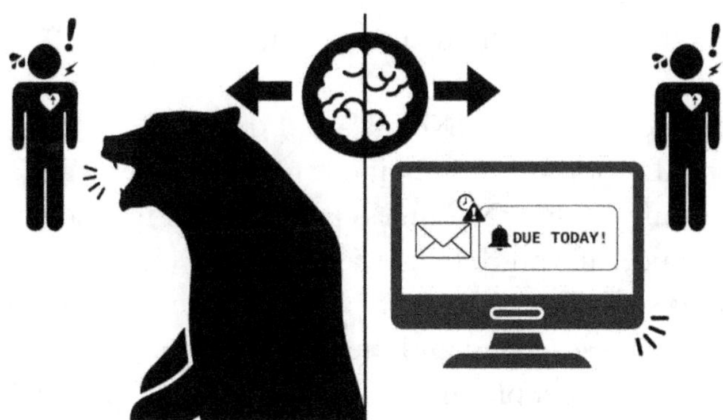

Figure 3.1: Stress response from real or perceived threat

It's not just wild animals that have us beat on the stress-disease-performance front. Our ancestors probably suffered from fewer stress-related disorders than we do. While they lived in harsh and dangerous environments, they did not experience the constant psychological strain that we face today. Where our forebearers faced animals with big teeth and claws, we deal with things like over-packed schedules, complex social expectations, and FOMO, or Fear Of Missing Out. What's more, by fighting and fleeing, they used up much of the stress energy generated, and after the threat passed, they headed back to the cave to finish recovering. This full reset at the ANS level gave them even more capacity to face the next big challenge. This is resilience: growing our capacity for stress, not just bouncing back.

It is the accumulated burden from chronic (mainly psychological or emotional) stress that harms us, not stress itself. Today, we very rarely use up stress energy when dealing with our daily threats. Think of the last time you were really stressed at work. Did you get to chase off the "predator" or fight it out in hand-to-hand combat?

SERGEANT BACA AND 0-60

Think back to the story with Sergeant Baca in Chapter 2. After his buddies confirmed that throwing a chair truly *was* his first indication of stress, even though I knew the answer, I asked him, "So…do you get to throw the chair?

He chuckled and said, "No ma'am, I don't."

I asked, "Do you get to fight it out in some other way?"

"No ma'am, I don't. Not unless I want to get in trouble."

"So," I said, "if you don't get to throw the chair or run off your anger, who is suffering, you or the person you're so angry at?"

He paused for a second and then nodded his head. "I am."

He, like many people, had learned growing up that he had to "suck it up and drive on," that admitting stress was a sign of weakness, and that mental toughness and grit would see him through. We can grab stress by the shoulders, look it in the eye, and figure out if it's helpful or not. And if it's not, we should have the tools to deal with it. That's how we build resilience, not by denying and carrying on until it overtakes us.

In case you're not yet convinced why it's worth learning to recognize a stress response early and then using the tools to modulate it, let me share this with you.

We've established that stress is not inherently good or bad, but the type of stress we have to manage (chronic psychosocial or emotional stress) is more complex to recover from than physical stress. Plus, we're not even close to fully recovering, given the back-to-back stressors we face. There is no time to "run back to our cave" and rest for a day to allow the stress energy to discharge. Unless we're consistently working at the level of the ANS, we're basically papering over the problem.

As a result, the ANS is idling at high revs much of the day, on most days, as stressors continue to stack up. We need to not only allow the system to downshift to a lower idling rev but also tune up our engine, moving it into a higher-performing state. Enhancing our interoceptive awareness and using that knowledge to fully modulate the ANS (dial up or down our stress level) is how we continue to tune up our systems moment by moment, day by day.

Thankfully, most of us don't get to the point where our first indication of feeling stressed is that we have to fight the urge to pick up a chair and throw it at somebody, but that doesn't mean we, our team members, and our organization are not suffering in some ways from the constant onslaught of stress that goes unnoticed, unchecked, and unregulated.

Chronic stress depletes our physiological resources, leading to exhaustion, cynicism, and disengagement. It can lead to toxic leadership and work cultures because chronically stressed leaders are more reactive. They may become more controlling to manage their internal chaotic environment or to avoid engaging with people, becoming robotic. In either case, employee engagement and motivation will suffer. Given that workplaces are human systems and chronic, unmanaged stress disrupts them, it stands to reason that unregulated stress has a significant impact on workplace performance and resilience. But there is a way through this, and it comes down to giving the brain-body system what it needs: full recovery from stress.

What do we do about this chronic stress that the vast majority of us deal with? How do we tap into this natural process of interoception and build our interoceptive awareness so we reach the point of using our stress energy wisely and well and learn to recover fully? The process isn't necessarily easy to master right away, since we're building new habits and capacities, but it follows a pretty simple formula.

Start by practicing tuning into the body whenever you can. Pause for five to ten seconds (or more). Don't wait until you are in a high-stress situation. Do it when you wake up or when you sit down to eat or drink something. Just notice what you become aware of.

- Engage with a coach, therapist, mind-body practitioner, or other qualified professional to learn to accurately interpret what the body signal is saying. Consistently practice techniques that directly modulate (dial up or down) stress.
- Get clear on your stress triggers. What causes you to feel stress?
- Keep practicing tuning into the body. Make a list of signs of stress and see if you can link them to triggers.

- Become aware of signature signs of stress. Which signs show up time and time again?

Throughout this process, there are awareness-building opportunities, such as:

1. When we notice these first signs of stress
2. When we try to figure out what caused the stress response
3. When we decide whether we have a helpful level of stress (Is it supporting our performance goals or compromising our ability to think clearly, make good decisions, communicate clearly, etc.?)

It's amazing how much we can learn about ourselves from one short practice. Like any capacity or skill, though, this is an ongoing process of development.

Important note: Ideally, you will have a qualified professional to guide you from the beginning. When it comes to regulating stress in the body (i.e., physiologically, which gets to the foundational part of the stress-response-recovery system), it is important to have a good coach or trainer. They will help you accurately interpret the bodily signals and guide you through appropriate and effective techniques to recover and utilize the resulting self-knowledge for future learning, decision-making, and myriad choice points. Scan the QR code at the beginning or end of this book to contact us and find a qualified coach.

For purposes of illustration, imagine you're in a meeting, standing your ground on something you feel strongly about. The debate is going well for you, and you feel energized, excited, and motivated to get your points across clearly. After about 20 minutes, however, you notice that your thinking gets a little fuzzy, you feel a buzzing or tingling in your body that wasn't there before, you have a bit more trouble communicating succinctly, and you feel deflated. You will likely have gone from just the right level of stress activation to too much.

I want to help people reach the point where they recognize and learn their bodily signals associated with different stress-activation levels. What is happening in the body when thinking is fuzzy and slow versus clear and quick? How does your body tell you that you are experiencing anxiety versus excitement? What about resignation versus motivation, or apathy versus passion? For many, just knowing about these differences intellectually doesn't mean they'll immediately be able to feel sensations in the body that accompany thinking or cognitive performance.

Stress doesn't always come in loud and obvious ways. It can be insidious, often quietly building in such a way that we don't realize what is happening, like water dripping into a bucket. All seems well until it overflows. Sergeant Baca was likely experiencing stressor after stressor, without sufficient regulation, long before he wanted to grab a chair. He, like many people that I have worked with, wasn't aware of stress until it became a problem. Because of its prevalence and its role in our functioning, it behooves us to understand how it shows up, when it's helpful or harmful, and how to manage it effectively.

We want to manipulate our stress level enough to complete our tasks, meet our goals, and be at our best as much as possible.

LEARN TO INTERPRET THE BODY-BRAIN LANGUAGE (WITH A QUALIFIED COACH!)

Once my clients can notice bodily sensations associated with stress, I help them interpret those signals accurately for the situation and use that newfound knowledge and wisdom to take smart steps and intelligence that involve the body. I work with them to incorporate this enhanced capacity into their daily lives. This is the secret sauce to better overall performance and well-being. We work with the core elements of our functioning.

As part of our work, we also examine what creates a stress response for us. What causes me to feel stressed isn't the same for others. Additionally, what frustrates me one day may not bother me at all on another. There are a number of reasons for this, including how well we are sleeping, eating, hydrating, and moving our bodies. These are all sources of stress on the system. We might wake up with an elevated stress level even before our child wakes up with a fever, or we leave late for work only to discover the roads are backed up, the bus is late, or the metro line is shut down.

During a typical day, how often do you truly take time to fully reset between one demand and the next? If you are a team lead or manager, do you encourage your people to reset between challenges? Or do you assume they know how to take care of themselves, and as long as they show up and do their jobs, all is well?

We need our go-to relaxation strategies: working out, reading, watching a show, spending time with our families or pets, and vacationing. These activities matter, and they do bring some relief from the day-to-day stressors. However, they are often insufficient to bring the nervous system back to baseline. We are tricked into thinking that relaxation is enough recovery. Why? We often lack a clear understanding of the full recovery process from psychological stress.

To illustrate what I mean, consider the stress we experience from an intense workout. After we finish a long run or HIIT class, we have to do more than rest or relax. Full recovery requires our bodies to repair and restore balance throughout the system. When we get this level of recovery, we're stronger and more fit to move to the next level of intensity. This is the same for psychological stress. Full recovery from the stress we experience in our daily lives only happens when the brain-body system returns to a balanced state of homeostasis, achieved at the nervous system level.

Ideally, we will not just "get through" tough days or weeks. We want to grow more resilient because of them, not inch our way to burnout. The only way to become more resilient is to fully recover from the stress activation. When we do, we are ready to face even bigger and more frequent challenges later. Let's look at how we can train ourselves to get a full recovery.

The majority of popular articles and mainstream conversation on stress and emotion regulation either revolve around cognitive strategies (reframing, positive self-talk, and perspective shifts); social strategy (e.g., having a pint at the pub with a mate, having a long chat with a friend, joining a group or club based on special interests); or passive strategies (reading a good book, watching a movie, or taking a hot bath).

From my work as a psychotherapist and an avid consumer of cognitive and neuroscience research, I understand the value of these techniques; I use them myself and teach them in my courses and coaching sessions. I also understand the main reasons they are considered go-to approaches for managing our stress. One is that they are based on cognitive-behavioral therapy, which is the most popular and widely researched psychotherapeutic modality, especially in the high-income Western world. Another is that they are relatively easy to grasp because they align with Western philosophy, which holds that thinking defines the essence of who we are, as expressed by René Descartes in the 1600s: "I think, therefore I am."

The issue isn't that these strategies aren't helpful; they are. But relying on them neglects the role of the body in our stress response and the fact that our thoughts and perceptions come after. So, if we want to catch the *influencer* of our thoughts; we need to pay attention to the body. It's very difficult to take control of thoughts while the body and brain are still in stress mode.

Therefore, the most effective strategy is to combine all of these strategies. Including body-based stress regulation techniques, such as interoceptive awareness, is a sure-fire way to make the other strategies much more effective and efficient. This is supported by a growing body of research telling us that sensing the body, accurately interpreting these sensations, and taking direct action to down-regulate the ANS are key to stress resilience, sound decision-making, and well-being. Since stress and emotion first show up in the body, why wait until they make their way up into our thoughts, moods, and other mentally influenced constructs?

A POWERFUL STRESS-MODULATION TOOLKIT

What we need is a toolkit that allows us to use our stress effectively and efficiently as the potentially productive energy source it is. We can, and should, carry this toolkit with us at all times so that we can pull it out at any time of the day, at work, at home, in a grocery store, on a train, and even during a conversation. We don't want to wait until we finish our workday, get to the weekend, or go on vacation before we address our stress load. By waiting even until the end of the day, we're back to coping with or managing our stress rather than modulating it.

After all, our ANS doesn't wait to function until we're done with a task. It is constantly working to keep us in balance. The two branches continuously engage in a lovely dance, with one leading (more dominant) and the other following (less dominant), then switching. This brilliant system is constantly working to allow us to meet the demands of the situation. Even when we are at rest, they alternate, shifting back and forth from milliseconds to minutes as they adjust according to what is happening in our bodies and what is going on outside of them. Once we learn to read our bodies' signs, adjust, and let our ANS do what it wants, we will be in a much better state for much longer.

Based on decades of studying, practicing, teaching, and coaching in human performance and well-being, it is clear to me that if we can start with a foundation in interoceptive awareness and apply our most effective psychological (cognitive) strategies, we will be able to modulate stress in the moment, rather than waiting until the end of the day, week, or month. If we bring our toolkit with us, we're more able to benefit from exercise, social, and passive approaches to "top off" our energy tank.

Figure 3.2: Stress-modulation toolkit

There are two helpful ways to improve awareness of bodily sensations, which is one of the two key aspects of interoceptive awareness. One is through contemplative practices such as certain mindfulness practices (body scan, awareness of breath, mindful walking, mindful eating), contemplative yoga, Tai Chi, and Qigong. Another is through Somatic Experiencing. These approaches encourage us to tune into the body and pay attention to the sensations. What they do not support is the interpretation of those sensations we're noticing. This cognitive process is not part of their approach. However, they are very helpful in raising our awareness of bodily sensations and in using that awareness in specific ways that align with their intended outcomes. Although it is beyond the scope of this book to go into the goals of these approaches and practices, it is worth looking into. Scan the QR code or contact me through my website if you are interested in how mindfulness practices or other somatic approaches can help you.

Research and our personal experience tell us that we are likely suffering from more extreme chronic stress than previous generations. This then becomes a serious issue for our organizations because we bring our entire system to work: our brain, our mind, and our bodies. And what many don't realize is that we carry residual stress in our bodies. So, again, the whole person shows up at work, and the whole person has likely experienced a lot of stress. Therefore, if we want high-functioning teams and support employee well-being, we would do well to provide the most solid support for understanding stress, recognizing it as soon as it shows up in the body, learning techniques to modulate it, and integrating all of this into the organizational culture.

The key to personal resilience and a thriving workplace is not eliminating stress and making everything comfortable. In fact, the goal should never be not to have stress. We need stress. The goal is to be aware of the stress response in the moment and to consciously and intelligently decide if it is working in our favor or not. If not, the goal then shifts to modulating the stress response to restore our equilibrium.

What we want is to be able to modulate our level of stress so that we have the right amount of energy for the requirements of the task or event, and then fully recover. This is just like manipulating the accelerator and brake pedals of a vehicle to reach our destination safely with the least wear and tear on the engine.

I want to help employees and teams use and modulate stress effectively by providing them the framework, techniques, tools, and environment to do that. In my decades of working with people to enhance their cognitive and physical resilience, their full range of intelligences, and their overall well-being, and by consuming hundreds of scientific papers and books on these topics, I am very confident that the most efficient and effective way to do this is by teaching them how to build a foundation of interoceptive awareness. This building block is a force multiplier for any development effort in your organization.

Chapter Four

THE ROLE OF INTEROCEPTIVE AWARENESS IN INTELLIGENCE

"Yesterday I was clever, so I wanted to change the world. Today I am wise, so I am changing myself."
—attributed to Jalal ad-Din Rumi (renowned Persian poet, jurist, and Islamic scholar)

KEY TAKEAWAYS:

- Intelligence is not fixed, nor can it accurately be captured in a single score.
- Our ability to modulate stress and emotions is closely tied to our ability to fully utilize our intelligence.
- Intelligence is not limited to brain activity but emerges from a dynamic relationship between the brain, the body, and the environment.

This chapter explores how interoceptive awareness provides a solid foundation for our full range of capacities and sustained, high-level performance. We'll start by unpacking what makes up someone's ability to learn, adapt, solve problems, and work well with others, so we don't just have a lot of individual stars but a cohesive, high-functioning team. Establishing the range of our intelligences (yes, plural) is a crucial part of understanding why interoceptive awareness is so important to using our capacities.

HOW DO YOU IDENTIFY INTELLIGENCES?

Let's try a short thought experiment.

Try to think of someone that you would describe as very intelligent. How does that person demonstrate their intelligence? Where did their intelligence come from?

If you are a hiring manager, what are you looking for in a candidate? Do you assess intelligence through an aptitude or reasoning test or through inference? Or do you assume intelligence based on their CV?

What types of intelligence are you either openly seeking or quietly trying to assess? How influenced is your organization (and you personally) by the dominant idea of intelligence, measured by a quotient? Or is your focus based on relevant skills and experience outside of any traditional framework?

When I ask people to describe someone they consider to be very intelligent, I usually get responses like, "She knows a lot about ________!" or "They are great at math," "He has an incredible memory," or "She is so logical."

It is less common to hear famous athletes, dancers, artists, musicians, public speakers, and writers described as superintelligent. Similarly, I rarely hear people describe entertainers or business leaders as intelligent, even when their success clearly depends on sophisticated interpersonal and emotional intelligence or timing in telling a joke or making decisions about product marketing. Instead, they are said to be "great" at what they do. Just as language reflects and influences our ideas about stress, resilience, well-being, and performance, it likewise reveals a lot about how we view intelligence. How many times have you heard (and perhaps used) phrases such as "Well, I am (she is, he is) no Einstein," "Use your head!" or "You do the math"?

Being good with numbers and science, recalling information on the fly, and getting good grades are, of course, indications of intellectual capacities, but they are only some of the ways we express intelligence. However, despite significant movement in psychology away from a narrow definition of intelligence, namely IQ, there is a prevailing belief that intelligence is demonstrated by our school grades (called *marks* in non-U.S. countries), how quickly we think or solve problems, and how well we easily recall facts and figures.

This view, while narrow, is not surprising. Human intelligence is so complex that even after it has been scientifically studied for over 200 years, we are still learning much about it. Over the past century, our collective understanding of who is "smart" has largely been shaped by a single psychometric assessment: the Stanford-Binet Intelligence Quotient (IQ) assessment.

This test is, in fact, not based on a theory of intelligence; rather, it is a functional, practical way to quickly assess someone's intelligence in a controlled setting for defined applications. It gained traction, not because it accurately reflected the wide range of human intelligences, but because it was easy to administer and aligned with the prevailing scientific views of the time. Furthermore, it efficiently met institutional needs, including placing students, making hiring decisions, screening immigrants, and quickly assessing the mental ability of military recruits starting in WWI.

Alfred Binet, who developed the first intelligence test, never intended his work to be used to define and assign a number that would describe our full intellectual capacity. In 1904, he was commissioned by the French Ministry of Education to find a way to determine whether children struggled in school due to low ability or insufficient instruction. Its goal was to figure out which children needed additional academic support, not to define intelligence as innate and fixed. Binet was, in fact, critical of how his work ended up being used. In his 1909 book *Modern Ideas About Children* (translated version of *Les Idées Modernes sur les Enfants*), he railed against the misuse of his assessment being used to support "... deplorable verdicts that an individual's intelligence is a fixed quantity, a quantity which cannot be increased. We must protest and react against this brutal pessimism."

Yet the standardized IQ test continues to prop up our general idea that we are born with a fixed intelligence that shows up in specific (and narrow) ways. I am not suggesting that the capacities targeted in standardized IQ tests don't measure *aspects* of intelligence. I argue that these tests cannot fully capture the various ways we demonstrate our intellectual capacities, which are just as important as those measured by the IQ test.

There are so many ways we demonstrate intelligence that, as Howard Gardner, developer of the Multiple Intelligence Theory, claims, it's likely impossible to measure our full intelligence. Also, I argue (as many do) that these capacities are not fixed at birth; rather, they change over time and are influenced by environment, conditions, exposure, and practice. Such factors include how well we modulate our stress and how psychologically safe we feel in expressing our ideas and capabilities.

Thankfully, our perception of what constitutes intelligence is changing, albeit slowly. Particularly since the 1960s, a number of other theories and frameworks of intelligence have emerged, supporting us in stepping away from the belief that intelligence is fixed and narrow.

The first culturally seismic shift in perceptions of intelligence (at least in the United States) came from the publication of Daniel Goleman's book *Emotional Intelligence: Why It Can Matter More than IQ* (Goleman, 1995). Though Solovey and Mayer established the scientific foundation of emotional intelligence, Goleman's work got into our mainstream thinking.

In the early 2000s, another powerful framework emerged: cultural intelligence (CQ®). As stated on the Cultural Intelligence Center website (https://culturalq.com), "Cultural intelligence picks up where emotional intelligence leaves off and allows you to have the social sensibilities and practical skills to work and relate effectively with people from novel cultures." CQ is grounded in theories of intelligence, not just cultural sensitivity; it integrates cognitive understanding, metacognitive awareness, motivational engagement, and behavioral adaptability to enable more effective cross-cultural functioning.

More recently, psychologist Scott Barry Kaufman has proposed that we have a personal intelligence, which develops through the interaction between inborn cognitive (thinking, reasoning, intellectual) capacities and other dimensions such as self-awareness, emotional and stress regulation, motivation, and adaptability. Together, these frameworks indicate a move away from seeing intelligence as fixed, easily measured, and inborn. Instead, they, and the research behind these frameworks, suggest that our "intelligence" is an evolving capacity shaped by how we learn, relate, and grow through experience.

How is this all related to interoceptive intelligence? Modern research challenges the historic brain-centric view of intelligence. Studies show that our bodies actively contribute to thinking through interoceptive signals: the constant stream of information from our organs, muscles, and cardiovascular system that influences everything from intuitive decision-making to creative insight. Additionally, given the role of stress resilience in our ability to learn, grow, and adapt, I believe resilience enables us to more fully utilize and express our full range of intelligence. Resilience allows flexibility in our thinking, clarity in our decision-making, stabilization of our emotions, and adaptive relationships.

Advances in neuroscience expand our understanding of intelligence to include the role of the brain's capacity for adaptation, regulation, and connection in the expression of our intelligence. Emerging research helps us better understand that intelligence is influenced by how our brain-body system interacts to respond to stress, process (and use) emotions, and adapt to changing conditions.

We are starting to see intelligence as more personally unique and dynamic, driven by the bidirectional influence between ability and engagement as we pursue our goals. Engagement is strongly impacted by how we regulate our stress, which depends on our ability to tune in and self-regulate through interoceptive awareness.

A growing body of research indicates that our ability to regulate stress and emotions is closely tied to our ability to fully utilize our intelligence. And here, once again, we bump up against a limited view that hinders us. Because of cognitive behavioral therapy's strong foundation, there is widespread belief that stress resilience is achieved through cognitive strategies that use our minds to shift us from a high-stress to a regulated state. That can work, depending on the person using this technique regarding their history and their level of dysregulation. My work with the military, wildland firefighters, first responders, and people with certain trauma histories has shown me that asking certain people to regulate their stress through their thoughts can set them up to fail.

Instead, I find that the best results come from an integrative approach, one that is based on how a person's entire system works together in a brain and mind-body system. The most efficient and effective self-regulation and stress modulation come when we *combine* neurophysiological, cognitive self-regulation, and mindfulness techniques.

All of this comes down to widening our view of the different types and manifestations of intelligence, as well as the role our capacity to read bodily signals plays in expressing our overall intelligence. We are on the way to integrating interoceptive awareness into the framework of intelligence. In fact, research indicates that interoceptive awareness is foundational to our ability to access and express our intelligence.

I propose considering a type of "intelligence wheel," as illustrated in Figure 4.1. While this intelligence wheel illustration doesn't capture all the ways we likely manifest intelligence, it offers a much more inclusive view of our vast range of being smart and the role interoceptive awareness may play in it.

INTELLIGENCES

Adaptive	• Learning from feedback & experience • Adjusting strategies in dynamic conditions • Integrating multiple forms of knowledge (cognitive, emotional, contextual) • Maintaining effectiveness under stress or ambiguity
Body-Based (Kinesthetic)	• Using internal states as knowledge • Using body with precision, control & skill • Embodied decision-making and intuition • Using body for "knowing" and predicting
Cognitive	• Logical reasoning & problem-solving • Working memory & information processing • Verbal & mathematical proficiency • Abstract & conceptual thinking
Cultural	• Understanding norms & practices across cultures • Awareness of assumptions & planning for interactions • Maintaining interest, confidence & interest in other cultures • Adapting verbal/nonverbal acts to fit cultural context
Emotional	• Emotional awareness & labeling • Self-regulation & impulse control • Empathy & perspective-taking • Navigating emotionally charged situations effectively
Personal	• Self-reflection & self-knowledge • Goal alignment & meaning-making • Life narrative construction (understanding personal growth and identity) • Integrating strengths and managing inner conflict
Social	• Reading nonverbal cues & social dynamics • Understanding social roles and norms • Influencing & collaborating with others • Building and maintaining relationships

Figure 4.1: Interoceptive awareness: the hub of the intelligence wheel

As Rolf Pfeifer and Josh Bongard argue in *How the Body Shapes the Way We Think: A New View of Intelligence* (Pfeifer and Bongard 2006), intelligence is not limited to brain activity but emerges from a dynamic relationship between the brain, the body, and the environment. Interoceptive awareness is central to that relationship. It allows us to more effectively determine whether we are in a state of stress energy that supports the best decisions, clearest thinking, greatest adaptability, optimal curiosity, strong motivation, creative problem-solving, appropriate empathy, perspective-shifting, and more. High interoceptive awareness allows us to access our gut instincts and integrate them with our cognitive processing to arrive at the best decision for the situation.

In the next six chapters, we'll look at real-life examples of when our inability to watch our bodies and listen to the conversation between the body and brain blocks us from using our full range of intelligences. These case studies are not unique, even though they may appear to be somewhat extreme. I chose them because, based on what I have seen in my work, the underlying causes of problems illustrated in these cases are very common; they all come from a lack of awareness of what is going on in our brain and mind-body systems, and this lack of awareness disconnects us from our values, our goals, and our capacities to be who we *can* be.

Let's now dive into case studies of people, teams, and organizations that were seriously struggling because of a lack of understanding of stress and how to modulate it. I worked with them to raise the tide of performance by blending coaching and training in interoceptive awareness with other frameworks and approaches to enhance human performance.

Chapter Five

THE ROI OF SHOWING APPRECIATION

"Leadership is about taking responsibility for lives and not numbers."
—Simon Sinek (leadership expert, author
best known for his book *Start With Why)*

KEY TAKEAWAYS:

- Low interoception is linked to weaker emotional and social attunement, which can make connection with others more difficult.
- Demonstrating authentic appreciation boosts company productivity and profit.
- We are most effective as leaders when we lead from the heart (body) as much as the head (brain).
- Blending interoceptive awareness with mindfulness and cognitive strategies is a very effective approach for people who are primarily comfortable living in their heads (cognitive processing).

I worked with a skincare company whose mission was to help women feel good in their own skin at any age. With boutique-style stores, they were known for exceptional personalized service, high-quality products, and loyal clientele. During the COVID-19 pandemic, their brick-and-mortar sales plummeted while online sales soared. While they were grateful for the continued sales, even a year post-COVID, it was clear the business model had changed.

As part of the transition to a new model, the CEO brought in Angie, a rising star in the Silicon Valley tech world. She was well known for her keen analytical mind and her ability to use data-driven techniques to maximize performance. She seemed to be just the right person to help them figure out how to manage this transition. The executive team assumed that Angie's way of thinking and knowledge of analytics would translate into promoting scale and efficiency in the post-COVID marketplace.

Similar to her approach in Silicon Valley, Angie focused more on predictive analytics and key performance indicators than on human resources. To increase productivity, she set new (and challenging) sales goals and applied her analytical reasoning to optimize procedures. She cut staff in the physical stores but told the remaining associates they needed to continue to provide the same level of customer service as in years past, despite the lower headcount.

PROBLEM

While the employees who survived the cuts were happy to have a job, they weren't sure how to maintain the previous level of personalized customer service and handle all other store-related tasks. They were running ragged. While they didn't mind hard work, it felt as if their efforts were expected but not valued.

Angie had failed to notice an important distinction between the company's culture and her approach to business. She valued sales figures, headcount, projections, and company performance reports instead of talking to her staff to learn about their goals and challenges. But the company's success was based on more than hitting sales targets. It also came from building and nurturing relationships in the organization and between clients and sales staff.

Within six months, employees felt like nothing more than entries on a spreadsheet. Their opinions were disregarded in favor of data models, and impersonal quarterly reviews replaced discussions about personal growth. The company's historically enthusiastic and devoted sales force started to retreat.

Despite the attrition, Angie appeared to have little empathy or ability to connect with her downline managers, much less to deal with the challenges faced by those responsible for sales in the stores. The staff felt that Angie's leadership didn't acknowledge their efforts or address their concerns or the stress of covering additional tasks due to staffing reductions while meeting customer needs. Morale was low, and burnout risks mounted. Absenteeism increased, and when employees were at work, they wondered if the effort was worth it. Engagement suffered.

SOLUTION

I took a two-pronged approach. For the sales associates, my first step was to assess their perceived stress, how they viewed the sources of that stress, and which behavioral and other indicators they believed would indicate an engaged, authentic leader. We explored the role of trust and the factors that impacted their motivation and commitment to the organization. We met weekly to enhance their interoceptive awareness. We started with body-based (neurophysiological) self-regulation techniques for a few weeks, then added cognitive strategies, and eventually brought in mindfulness work.

While working with the sales associates, I provided individual coaching to Angie. We explored her personal and professional goals, her frustrations, and her stressors. Given her appreciation for science, I based most of our discussions on neuroscience and explained the role of interoception in our functioning, as well as how humans are *wired* for needs such as social connection and safety. We also discussed the neuroscience of motivation, engagement, and feeling valued, as well as the importance of trust.

It came out in our sessions that she was having health issues that were exacerbated by stress, so I was able to loop that back into the conversation and give her a sense of the value of interoceptive awareness for catching stress early to support better health. Each session began with a focus on goals, followed by a conversation, interoceptive awareness exercises, and, eventually, the enhancement of emotional and social intelligence skills.

The sales staff needed two things:

1. Stress-modulation support
2. Signs that Angie and other leaders cared about them, which was key to getting back to the company culture they enjoyed and also their previous brand differentiator.

Leadership needed to understand, cognitively and then somatically (i.e., to *feel),* the benefits of authentic, embodied leadership. Through coaching and training in interoceptive awareness, Angie was able to see that disconnection with her body both caused and exacerbated her health issues. There is also often a bidirectional relationship between disembodiment (lack of body awareness) and a preference for cognitive information processing and decision-making. As she learned to better regulate her stress, her emotional intelligence grew, making it easier to expand her repertoire of leadership skills. In time, she came to understand and embody a more well-rounded style, one that incorporated her comfort in the quantitative realm with the newfound skill of a person-centered view.

OUTCOMES

By the end of our six-month engagement, sales staff were taking 65 percent less paid time off (and they admitted to taking mental health days just to get a break from the work environment). While the work demands remained the same, they felt like they were part of a mission. They also started to rekindle the pre-COVID connection with customers, something that had historically been correlated with high customer satisfaction. They no longer saw their customers as a source of stress and instead remembered to consider each interaction as an opportunity to reconnect with the reason they joined the company in the first place.

As I moved into the final phase of my work, I held team discussions with both the sales associates and Angie, which further reinforced a sense of *one team, one fight.* Surveys indicated greater work satisfaction among the sales associates, while 360-degree feedback for Angie indicated a significant improvement in how employees perceived her.

INSIGHTS

Leaders' level of interoceptive awareness will impact their emotional and social intelligence, as well as their ability to connect with others. Disembodiment (loss of body awareness) is common among people who value their cognitive capacities over connecting with others at an emotional level. It's important for a leader to pick up on emotional signals from their team and respond effectively. It doesn't mean coddling their sales staff nor pandering to emotional outbursts.

On the contrary, it's all about emotion regulation. What often surprises those who are highly dependent on cognition (an exaggerated version is Spock or Data from Star Trek) is that emotional intelligence is not about *giving in* to emotions or allowing them to run the show. It's also not about repressing them. Rather, it's about experiencing the full spectrum of emotions and not getting jerked around by them. We all experience emotions as humans; we just need to know how to use them as information, just like we need to learn how to use stress energy.

Interoceptive awareness is crucial because it allows us to perceive the signals between our bodies and brains, understand what they mean, and adjust accordingly for optimal social interactions, performance, and well-being.

All of this builds our capacity to know ourselves inside and out and better understand our needs and natural responses to being appreciated, valued, and seen. This, I argue, is as powerful as the biological needs for food, water, and shelter, because it's all about safety.

Leadership expert, economist, and retired U.S. Navy commander Mary Kelly discusses the importance of building trust and connecting authentically with teams to foster a trustworthy, productive work environment in her book *Why Leaders Fail: and the 7 Prescriptions for Success* (Stark and Kelly 2016). She, along with many other thought leaders, emphasizes the importance of authentic leadership: a genuine, trust-based relationship between leaders and their teams built on openness, empathy, and alignment of values. Research shows a strong link between authentic, embodied leadership, which includes demonstrating appreciation toward employees, and a host of downstream benefits to their organization.

And what organization, whether in the private or public sector, doesn't seek a good ROI? Whether it's a question of profit in a corporation, or readiness and mission effectiveness in the military and law enforcement, study after study shows that authentic leadership is key to success. Research also shows that authentic leadership is based on the core capacities of emotional intelligence, such as empathy, adaptability, and effective communication and conflict management. All of these competencies are shown to be enhanced by cultivating body awareness, a key element of interoceptive awareness.

This is a core aspect of our human condition: when we feel seen, valued, and appreciated, brain regions associated with motivation and reward are activated. When leaders show employees that they are appreciated and valued, they have more committed, motivated, and engaged team members who want to stay. In a 2022 study, McKinsey & Company found that the key reason employees leave jobs is feeling undervalued and unappreciated (McKinsey & Company 2021). They aren't the first, nor are they the only ones to show this. Several studies over the past five to ten years have identified what motivates good employees to stay put, and it's not about the paycheck.

As I write this, we're seeing big changes in the workforce situation in the United States with government layoffs, so concern over attrition might be somewhat lower than it was a few months ago. But no organization wants to lose good people, and when they feel valued, employees will not just want to stay longer; they'll be more engaged and higher performing.

I see true, authentic, and effective leadership as the ability to inspire, empower, and guide others toward a shared goal. This is built on people feeling seen, valued, and appreciated (Wong 2025; Newlands 2024). Gallup has been saying this for a long time. Their research shows that some of the primary ways that employees know they're valued and appreciated are through supportive relationships, recognition and praise, opportunities for growth, and clear expectations and purpose. Each of these is rooted in appreciation and trust. The most effective leaders balance business acumen with emotional intelligence, ensuring that both the mission and the people are prioritized.

Because it improves self-awareness, self-regulation, empathy, and decision-making, interoceptive awareness is fundamental to a leader's ability to embody the true essence of leadership. It's fundamental to their emotional intelligence. Leaders with strong interoceptive awareness can more easily recognize and understand changes in their own breathing, heart rate, and muscle tension, so they can catch their emotions as they arise, rather than react without thinking.

This skill improves self-control, enabling leaders to manage their attention, remain composed, and respond intelligently under duress. It also helps them feel less uncomfortable with emotions because they know they can regulate them. Therefore, there's less of a tendency for leaders to opt for a dominant cognitive or even robotic approach.

Interoceptive awareness improves empathic attunement because leaders who are conscious of their own emotional and physiological states are usually better able to read others' subtle emotional cues. Leaders establish psychologically secure workplaces where staff members feel appreciated, heard, and inspired to provide their best efforts. A supportive work environment, one that demonstrates authentic appreciation of employees and supports their well-being, enjoys higher productivity, higher profits, and higher retention rates. What's not to love about this?

REFLECTION QUESTIONS:

1. Does your leadership style have room for authentic connection?
2. How do you show your people that you value them?
3. What does it *feel* like to you (in the body) when others show they value you and appreciate your efforts?

Chapter Six

WORKPLACE WARS AND THE RETURN-TO-OFFICE TENSION

"Your core values are the deeply held beliefs that authentically describe your soul."
—John C. Maxwell (leadership expert, speaker, and bestselling author of books on personal and organizational growth)

KEY TAKEAWAYS:

- The post-pandemic return-to-office (RTO) challenge is representative of ideological disputes.
- Such ideological challenges impact team cohesiveness because they stem from values and identities people hold firmly.
- When we feel our values and identity are challenged, we go into threat mode and exhibit strong physiological and emotional reactions.
- Clarifying values as a team and improving interoceptive

awareness around ideological challenges improves team functioning.

Many of us are part of conversations these days that include comments like, "The return-to-office (RTO) mandate is just wrong!" or "I'm more engaged when I have some autonomy and know that my leaders trust me as a professional." On the other side, we hear, "How can we possibly be an effective organization if we're not all working in the same place?" or "Hybrid work ruins communication and teamwork!"

Since starting my professional life decades ago and working with the private and public sectors, I don't think I've seen an organizational shift as significant as the post-COVID debate of RTO versus a remote or hybrid work model. It has severely affected workplace structures and leadership strategies and, very importantly, employee expectations and workplace dynamics.

The personal experiences and resulting mindsets around this transformation of how we work and how we see our best way of working have created a deep divide between co-workers. As a result, we're seeing negative impacts on team cohesion, collaboration, organizational culture, and well-being.

Because this issue is so pervasive, I have engaged with a number of teams and organizations in different countries and have created the following case study. I will provide a general explanation of how I have worked with teams on this challenge, illustrate the benefits of integrating interoceptive awareness into other coaching and training frameworks, and share the outcomes.

PROBLEM

Many of my clients' organizations adopted a hybrid work model after the COVID pandemic, a flexible structure allowing employees to split their time between working remotely and on-site. They approached me due to a growing divide. They were those who were convinced that remote work improved their productivity and supported a better work-life balance, while others insisted that allowing co-workers to work from home negatively impacted communication, collaboration, productivity, and organizational culture. I suspect that we've all seen this workplace war in action.

Rather than focus on the factors that lead organizations to choose one model over another, this chapter explores contributors to the strong positions taken and how those differences of opinion are impacting team cohesiveness. But this phenomenon is not limited to the RTO debate. We are seeing increasing polarization among families, friend groups, organizations, and countries. So, while this composite case study focuses on teams within organizations, it's about what makes us rigid in our stances and how interoceptive awareness can help mitigate this trend.

Organizations face difficult decisions about RTO mandates versus a fully remote or hybrid work model. They face logical challenges, as well as cultural strain, trust gaps, and lower team cohesion either way. For employees, I find that most people firmly stand in one camp or the other, with few seeing both sides of the argument. While we can find research supporting each, a rigid stance on the subject is usually influenced more by emotional factors than data or logic. The reason, I believe, for this particular tug-of-war is the depth of what is underneath one's position. When identity, fairness, and autonomy are threatened, strong emotions rise up (whether we are conscious of them or not), typically anger, fear, defensiveness, anxiety, shame, and sadness.

Once we take a strong stance on a subject, it's difficult for us to budge because so much is riding on our position internally (i.e., in our own minds). One of my supervisors in my counseling-psychology internship knew this well. As a couples therapist, he said, "People don't want to take a stand against themselves." In other words, once we plant our stake in the ground, it takes a lot to pull it back up and plant it elsewhere.

My clinical supervisor's statement is powerful. It explains how we become increasingly entrenched in our positions over time, making it harder to shift perspective and see another's point of view. As Harvard psychologist Howard Gardner discusses in *Changing Minds*, since we don't adopt positions through logic alone, data rarely shifts perspective. Changing our (or someone else's) mind requires resonance (an emotional alignment with new ideas), presenting information in different ways, and addressing our resistances to change.

So let's say there is irrefutable evidence that going back to being in the office full-time leads to more productivity, team cohesion, well-being, and a better organizational culture, or the opposite, that allowing flexibility through a hybrid solution is better. It would still take a long time before the debate settled down into a new and productive normal. What would that be? Why would we get so emotional about whether or not we all agree that returning to the office full-time is the right thing to do? This process does involve some reason, but emotion plays a very important role, sometimes more important than logic and reason.

Here's why. First of all, our work structure is part of our identity, and being required to work within a different structure can feel threatening to that identity. Secondly, once we believe something, we become entrenched, and whether or not we realize it or want to admit it, our brains filter incoming data, choosing to keep information that confirms what we believe (cognitive bias) and ignore information that contradicts our preconceived notions and beliefs.

The brain has to filter information because there's far too much of it coming at us at any given time, which allows it to support our pre-existing beliefs and stances. I argue that as far as the brain knows, when we're feeling forced against our will one way or the other, we feel like we're under threat. While it may sound like an exaggeration, if you go deep inside the brain, changing our mind can feel like a survival issue, precisely because of the deep psychological and neurobiological mechanisms that protect our sense of identity, social belonging, and cognitive stability.

Admitting we're wrong, particularly regarding deeply held values, group memberships, and our expertise, threatens our identity. Think of the identity politics we're seeing more and more in the United States, which is akin to belonging to a tribe (which our brains process as a matter of safety). Since the brain resists contradiction (i.e., considering our position could be wrong), it's literally taxing the brain to change conclusions. It's much easier and takes a lot less brain energy to stick with an existing belief. For this reason, shifting our position on anything (and, in the case of office work, whether it's better to enforce RTO or allow flexibility) feels difficult, so we tend to stick with our familiar camp.

It is well known that our brains are constantly scanning for physical threats, and research shows that our brains are also constantly scanning for social threats. The brain regions involved in processing physical threats largely overlap with those engaged when we feel socially excluded, rejected, or threatened (Eisenberger and Lieberman 2004, 297-300). It's not a stretch, then, to consider that social safety (staying with our chosen tribe) is as important as physical safety.

Matthew Lieberman and Naomi Eisenberger, both at the University of California, Los Angeles, have been studying social isolation. Their findings indicate that when people feel excluded or dismissed, their brains register the experience as physical pain, which impacts morale, engagement, and performance. In Dr. Lieberman's book, *Social: Why Our Brains Are Wired to Connect*, it states that status, connection, and fairness all have demonstrable effects on the bottom lines of organizations, yet few take these issues seriously.

Why is feeling disrespected processed similarly to experiencing physical pain? Eons ago, being cast out of our tribe to fend for ourselves against large animals and other tribes very likely meant death. Our brain circuitry processes disrespect or feeling undervalued in the same basic way today.

When we take a position on an issue, such as an RTO policy, facing opposition can feel like a lack of respect. In Chapter 5, we saw how employees responded to feeling undervalued, and research tells us that the perception (or the reality) of being undervalued feels threatening. David Rock, co-founder and CEO of the NeuroLeadership Institute, has developed a model of the social concerns that drive our behavior. His model is based on an organizing principle of our brain: to minimize threat and maximize reward, and his research shows that there are at least five ways in which our brains either respond to a situation as threatening or as safe and rewarding.

Those five domains, designated by the acronym SCARF, are known as follows:

- Status (our relative importance to others)
- Certainty (our ability to predict the future)
- Autonomy (our sense of control over our life events)
- Relatedness (our sense of safety with others)
- Fairness (our perception of fair exchanges between people)

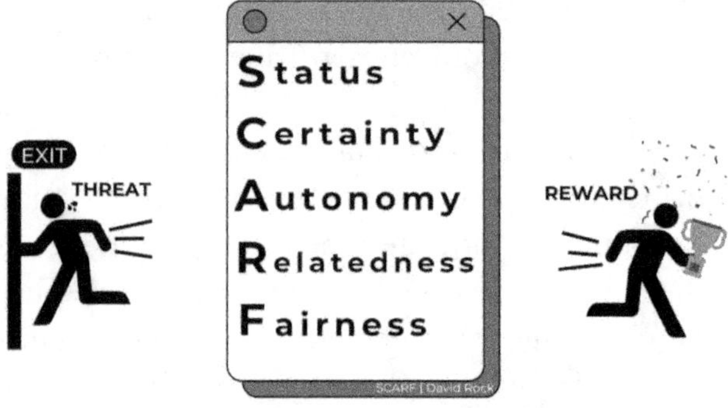

Figure 6.1: The SCARF model of social threats and rewards

Dr. Rock's research shows that we are usually triggered by more than one of these, and at work we are usually triggered by more than one at the same time. It makes sense that we would be triggered by threats within these domains, as they are all related to our sense of self: our personal, social, and professional identities. A threat to our sense of self activates our brain's threat response. In that moment, we are in survival mode.

It is widely accepted that when we have a threat response, whether it's from a physical or a social threat, real or perceived, we will have an emotional response, even if we aren't aware of it or have been trained to suppress it. Also, researchers in the fields of biology, neuroscience, psychology, and behavioral science tell us that emotions impact behavior. Being in a threat mode means we're not accessing our full capacity to think, process, make decisions, empathize, shift perspective, and communicate.

SOLUTION

With each of the teams I worked with, my first step was to explore their values, their identity (personal and professional), how they experienced and perceived stress, and, of course, their opinions about on-site versus remote work. Because most of us do not spend time thinking about this on our own, it is helpful to start with questionnaires to connect concepts to their internal experiences and create a baseline for outcome metrics.

We then focused on linking the benefits to stress regulation, mental flexibility, adaptability, communication, and capacities that support relationship building and psychological safety. We looked at the stress response in the brain-body system, talked about what real stress recovery is, and explored how to begin to recognize our signature signs of stress. Most importantly, we learned when we're experiencing a helpful level of stress or an unhelpful level, and how to manipulate that level so we can be at our best. We then moved on to techniques that help us interpret signals from the body to the brain, thereby building interoceptive awareness.

We used scenarios to practice self-regulation techniques. This gave them opportunities to practice responding more effectively when actual frustration, anger, or defensiveness arose while role-playing with people and situations that ran counter to values, identities, beliefs, wishes, and needs.

These types of learning conditions reinforce what it feels and looks like when we can generate a sense of calm, even during difficult discussions. We focused on the differences between states of calm and detachment. When emotions run high, it's not uncommon for people to emotionally detach to get by, as it is often a more socially acceptable response than showing emotion. We discussed the optimal range of emotional experience and expression for workplaces and their values.

We spent time exploring how interoceptive awareness allows us to tap into the continuous brain-body conversation that influences all of our human processes: thoughts, emotions, mindsets, openness, decisions, energy levels, well-being, and more. We discussed how awareness of those signals between the body and the brain helps us have more mental flexibility. We examined the normalcy of fear-based reactions when encountering someone whose beliefs or positions are at odds with our own.

The participants left with individual plans to integrate interoceptive awareness practices into their daily lives and to incorporate these practices into their organizational culture. They started and ended meetings with brief interoceptive awareness exercises, explored vocabulary, and found ways to normalize discussions about interoceptive awareness while supporting each other in capacity-building.

Next, we explored the SCARF model, our own triggers, and what a threat (stress) response feels like in those particular domains. We each have our own signs of what's going on in the situation that might have triggered the stress response, meaning when our brain is in threat mode, it can calm the system through interoceptive awareness practices and then reassess the situation.

Some think that we can only be productive when we're in the office together all of the time. So whether you're in an organization that has a mandate to go back to the office or you're still in an organization that allows some hybrid work, we know there will be people in our organizations, perhaps it's even us, who are unhappy. If we recognize that this unhappiness is our brain going into threat mode and employ techniques to down-regulate the response, we may be able to see the other camp's perspective more easily.

OUTCOMES

Post-training and coaching questionnaires showed a 68 percent increase (on average between the various groups) in their ability to detect early signs of stress and self-regulate (including their individual interoceptive awareness capacity). We saw on average a 72-percent increase in a sense of psychological safety and trust among the team members. Self-reports indicated greater adaptability, greater empathy, and greater ease in perspective shifting.

INSIGHTS

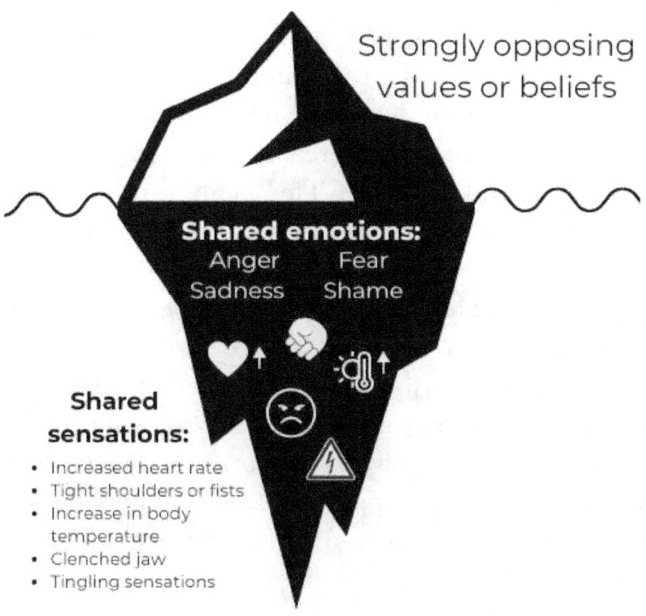

The challenges highlighted in this case study aren't limited to simply remote or hybrid work versus in-person work. As discussed, people and teams face "tribal" challenges anytime we're convinced that we're right about an adopted stance or when we feel deeply and passionately about a topic. It comes down to values and identity. When we encounter people who have beliefs or values that run counter to ours, our brain-body system will go into threat mode. If we're aware of the internal (bodily) signals of such a mode, we can more quickly assess and address the conflict. In fact, simply recognizing that someone on the other side of an issue is experiencing their own strong, internal experience better enables us to step back and consider what is going on underneath our stance. We see more clearly and can respond more effectively.

It's exhausting and unproductive to live in threat mode, especially when our lives are not truly at stake. So why not try to raise our awareness? And why not try to settle our brain-body system so we can open our minds to new ways of seeing, have greater empathy, and resolve these opposing-camp situations in a way that is respectful and productive?

Interoceptive awareness helps us identify the natural and instinctive responses that arise when we encounter new or difficult viewpoints and lays the groundwork for opening our minds. When we pay attention to how our bodies react to stress, we find some space between reaction and response. This enables us to pause, reflect, and approach a situation with interest rather than automatically defending our ideas.

In fact, there are almost no limits to the benefits of building our interoceptive awareness.

I have found that no matter what higher-level knowledge, skill, or ability I want to support in a group, starting with the foundation of interoceptive awareness always improves the process from start to finish. It makes any other approach easier to adopt and makes it stick a lot better. So when these organizations experienced polarization between an RTO and a hybrid or remote work model, I worked with them in the same way.

REFLECTION QUESTIONS

1. Can you recall a time when you felt you had no real choice over a decision that directly impacted you? What emotions or physiological (body-based) reactions did you have?
2. What triggers you the most? How might those triggers relate to your values?
3. When you are triggered by someone's words or actions, are you aware of any bodily signals indicating your brain is in threat mode?

Chapter Seven

SORTING OUT A BULLY LEADER

"Leadership is the capacity and the will to rally men and women to a common purpose and the character which inspires confidence."
—Field Marshal Bernard Montgomery, 1st Viscount Montgomery of Alamein, British Commander, World War II

KEY TAKEAWAYS:

- It can be difficult to distinguish between personality, cultural influences, and inappropriate behavior.
- A leader's past trauma can invade the workplace.
- Success when working with people from different cultures requires adaptability, flexibility, open-mindedness, and humility.

Having coached and trained many hundreds of civilians from across the professional spectrum and thousands of military personnel since 2007, if I were to ask twenty of them from each category to give me examples of what effective rallying looks like and what kind of character inspires confidence, I suspect a pattern would emerge. Sure, there would be variance among the responses by the military (especially between service branches) and civilians, but the differences *between* the military and civilian groups would probably be greater than within each category. Some leadership qualities might crossover between the two cultures, like integrity, but I have found that how strengths and characteristics are seen and valued generally differ between those who served in the military and civilians who have never served.

I chose the following case study because the situation could look very different depending on your (the reader's) personality, experiences, parenting, and culture. What is tough love to one person might be bullying to another. Of course, there are clear lines that should not be crossed in how we treat each other, but there is quite a bit of gray area, and often the fuzziness comes from cultural differences and a general lack of appreciation for how much this can challenge a team.

As you read through the case study, I encourage you to check in with your own thoughts, assumptions, judgments, and bodily sensations. Notice what you are thinking about, who you believe to be in the right and in the wrong, and why. The descriptions of what was going on for the key players are based on what I was told during our coaching, not my conjecture. I was called in to try to untangle a big mess and help the team hang on long enough to finish a project. I won't say it was easy, but it confirmed that even the most difficult and seemingly impossible situations can lead to growth.

I also chose this case study because it illustrates how a person's previous trauma underscores their need for interoceptive awareness and yet impedes it. It is an example of the complexity and the care taken when we're working with stress and trauma. In a sense, interoceptive awareness and the approaches I discuss all have the potential to, in essence, rewire our brains and nervous systems. Therein lies the power and the seriousness of the change process. This point reinforces my caution expressed in earlier chapters: that interoceptive awareness, as well as mindfulness and any body-based trauma-resolution approach, must be overseen by a qualified professional.

Let's meet Michael and his team.

Michael, a recently retired military officer, was brought into a small civilian organization to lead a small team tasked with developing a new training product for a large and important customer. The organization hoped that a successful delivery of this new product would lead to subsequent projects, giving them much-needed stability in a competitive market.

This was a challenging project for several reasons. The customer had a general vision for the final product (where and how it would be used) but had undefined requirements. As a result, the product development team faced significant uncertainty from the start. They felt like they were building the plane while flying it.

Also, the customer gave them a short turnaround time to deliver the beta version. While a few team members had experience with the product's target use, being the first training product of its kind, no one on the team had experience with the development tools required for the product. They weren't even sure whether or not the existing tools and platforms would meet their needs.

They were dealing with a complex situation. Thankfully, Michael's key personnel, Rachel and Miquela, fit that description. They had been hired onto the project around the same time and hit it off right away excited to work on a cutting-edge program. Both were energetic and had complementary skills. They believed in the mission and felt they had a solid team, not because of their experience (since no one actually had the necessary breadth of experience to develop a novel product), but rather because of their "can-do" attitude. They were more than willing to roll up their sleeves and make it happen.

PROBLEM

This was an exciting project and a valuable, positive learning and development opportunity for the organization, one that could catapult them into an entirely new area of expertise. A lot rode on the product's success. But, within a month of launching the project, excitement about this opportunity started to turn into a nightmare from two very different perspectives.

Michael managed the uncertainty by exerting control, maintaining a rigid hierarchy, and insisting on strict behavioral rules around status. He was the leader, and Rachel and Miquela were not. End of story. There was no room for discussions, negotiations, or creative thinking. These preferences may have come from inborn personality traits, childhood experiences, or having spent his entire adulthood to that point in the military. It most likely stemmed from more than one of these factors and was very likely exacerbated by the stress of the project (or chronic stress that might have been in his system for decades).

This leadership and management style didn't sit well with the team. Most of the members were on the project part-time, so Rachel and Miquela bore the brunt of Michael's severity and rigidity. Rachel and Miquela were civilians with extensive experience working with the military. They understood that the military and civilian cultures had many differences, but neither agreed that Michael's approach was appropriate or helpful for this particular situation.

Rachel and Miguela had formed a very tight unit, spending a fair amount of time laughing and eating lunch in one of their offices, behavior that Michael found childish and irritating. He interpreted their bond as a threat to his authority and attempted to create a wedge between them by pitting them against each other, trying to convince one to exclude the other, and became very angry when his attempts failed. This only caused them to form an even tighter bond, which infuriated Michael, and his behavior became more controlling and, they felt, threatening.

Despite this, Rachel and Miquela, along with the rest of the team, maintained their enthusiasm for the project. Their commitment never wavered in a successful, on-time delivery of the beta version. Michael, Rachel, and Miguela worked sixty to seventy hours per week, rarely taking a day off. Needless to say, their stress levels were high due to insufficient sleep and time to regulate. But they loved the project, and the work was not causing distress.

As far as the work was concerned, they were operating close to the optimal point on the Yerkes-Dodson U-shaped stress curve, but eventually they began to show signs of stress. However, it wasn't the long hours that started to wear them down but instead a growing fear, anger, and resentment toward Michael, whom they felt was creating a toxic work environment.

From Michael's perspective, Rachel and Miquela were overly sensitive, inefficient, and poor at following directions. He felt they were acting like upstarts who didn't know their place and didn't respect his authority. He went so far as to claim that they were deliberately sabotaging the product when a mistake was made by a subordinate team member under Rachel's direction.

While the project continued on schedule, the work environment became untenable for Rachel and Miquela. They both threatened to leave the project despite a looming delivery date unless the company owner took measures to address what they considered to be bullying behavior.

From Michael's perspective, it was his right to demand respect for his position, and that he was simply doing what he felt was necessary to keep the project on schedule. He would have preferred to bring in replacements who understood and accepted his leadership style. However, bringing two new people up to speed, albeit people who came from a similar work culture, would delay the project. So, he agreed to have someone come in to help the team cross the finish line.

Despite the issues, everyone on the team cared about the company's reputation and took pride in delivering a good product on time, so Rachel and Miquela agreed to stay on, with the caveat that Michael would agree to coaching.

That's when I entered the scene.

SOLUTION

If I were to move from the United States to, say, France or Malaysia, I would be expected to learn the customs of my adoptive country, the language, its values and how they are manifested, the expected behaviors in different circumstances, and so on. Assimilation is expected of expats who plan to integrate into the local community. The same is true of organizational, professional, and other subcultures, such as the general contrasts between military and civilian cultures. When I started working with the military, I learned as much as I could, just as I had when I was planning to live in French and Chinese cultures. The same was true for Michael, who had come to work for a civilian company. Even though the company's founder and some employees were former military, it was a civilian company operating in a civilian world.

This was important for me to establish right from the start with Michael. It wasn't a question of whether his behavior constituted bullying (that fell to HR, the company owner, and any legal counsel they might seek). The case before me involved cultural and value differences, as well as what was considered acceptable and unacceptable behavior, and what constituted good leadership in the civilian world, based on the trends and standards of the time (early 2020s).

This was my starting point with Michael. The phrase I mentioned in Chapter 4, "No one wants to take a stand against themselves," applies here. My goal was for Michael to be willing to consider whether his leadership and project-management style were effective in a civilian subculture, regardless of whether or not Rachel and Miquela were being disrespectful. Therefore, it was crucial that he not feel I was asking him to take a stand against himself.

It turned out that Michael sensed he was not being effective. However, he wasn't able to shift his thinking or his habitual responses, given the level of stress he was experiencing. Remember, he was not only dealing with the stress of the project's demands but also the stress he had brought with him from his past career. He was open to considering new ways of leading, as he wanted to stay on the project and with the company (motivation is a powerful thing!).

First, though, he and I needed to have conversations about stress, going way back. We weren't going to be able to bring about real change by focusing only on the stress and his reactions during the previous few months. He was open to that, and we were able to discuss the messages he received throughout his life about being mentally and physically tough. We contrasted his previous beliefs with biological resilience, which relates to adaptability, something he valued. We spent two months working twice a week on stress-regulation techniques, starting with interoceptive awareness, then body-based regulation, and finally cognitive strategies. I did not use the third tool of mindfulness in the kit, since he needed to focus on his interoceptive awareness and self-regulation for a longer period before we could consider introducing it.

While working with Michael, I was doing individual coaching with Rachel and Miquela. Their interoceptive awareness was quite high, so we were able to move quickly to body-based and cognitive self-regulation, focusing on those tools weekly for a month before introducing mindfulness.

After two months of individual work with Michael, Rachel, and Miquela, we were ready to bring everyone back together as a large group (including the other team members less affected by the dynamics with Michael) to explore values and begin examining the challenges and opportunities inherent in cultural differences.

I used the model of cultural intelligence (CQ) to build on the awareness gained from the interoceptive awareness techniques and values exploration. Next, we incorporated the concept of cultural intelligence, focusing on how we strategize in each moment to engage effectively with someone from a different background. This is a type of metacognition, meaning "thinking about our thinking." We practiced examples of how, when we're talking to someone from another culture or subculture (like military to civilian), we strategize in the moment as we notice whether something lands, if the person seems resistant, and all the ways we adapt to engage more effectively with them.

So, although the issues between Michael and the team were not limited to military and civilian cultural differences, this provided a foundation for further exploration. Michael's issues were more than just a cultural clash and not something that we could completely address in our setting, but we were able to build enough of a bridge that the team could complete the first phase of the project and move into the second.

OUTCOMES

Interviews with team members indicated that they each benefited personally from the work that we had done. Even Michael confirmed that the sessions helped him patch things up enough to get through the critical alpha and beta phases and to win the follow-on contract, which was a huge coup. Three of the seven team members left after the final product was delivered, but they felt that what they learned from the entire process was beneficial, and they went to their next jobs more resilient and better informed about themselves and the factors that impact their well-being and performance.

The good news wasn't only that the project was delivered on time, which was fabulous for the company, but that, out of the chaos and turmoil, three people emerged much better equipped to handle anything that came their way, more effectively, robustly, and resiliently.

INSIGHTS

Whenever there are problems between two or more people, we can assume that there are some cultural or value differences. And research shows that when our values are threatened, when someone behaves in a way that goes against them, we go into a threat response. When we have this normal reaction, there are three (some say four) options: fight, flight, or freeze (and fawn). In the case presented above, everyone spent most of their time in fight mode.

Just as I've been making the case that awareness is key to resolving stress-related issues, awareness is what we need to keep a difficult work situation from becoming toxic. The sooner we catch a stress response, the more power we have to understand it, and the more control we have over how to use it. I know the work that went into getting Michael, Rachel, and Miquela to step back, reflect, learn, and grow. There were times I was not at all sure they would come out of the situation unscathed. But we can't fix what we can't see. We must bring stress and emotion out of the shadows and into the light because they are in there, operating and impacting us regardless. I vote for awareness.

REFLECTION QUESTIONS:

1. Have you noticed any cultural differences in your organization?
2. Do you leverage those differences or hope they resolve themselves?
3. How will you know if and when behavior starts to turn toxic?

Chapter Eight

GOING FROM BURNOUT TO BALANCE

"A jug fills drop by drop."
—attributed to Siddhartha Gautama (The Buddha)

KEY TAKEAWAYS:

- You don't have to be in a life-threatening job to live with high stress; many people carry chronic stress from ordinary pressures without even knowing it.
- Chronic stress can lead to physical and mental health risks.
- Disengagement can result from stress-related exhaustion, low motivation, or a lack of interest.
- Improvements in interoceptive awareness can have a positive ripple effect on those around us.

While the adapted quote from Buddha above refers to good deeds accumulating drop by drop, the same applies to stress, which often accumulates drop by drop, outside of our awareness, until it spills over the edge.

I have worked with thousands of people who work in dangerous, life-threatening conditions, such as first responders, wildland firefighters, and the military. I have also worked with hundreds of people in jobs that wouldn't be considered life-threatening but could be in the long term. Many of them work very long hours in environments that are psychologically and emotionally, and sometimes physically, demanding. They have chosen these fields because they are committed to the mission, which drives them to keep at it even when they are suffering. They're not under fire like my military, firefighting, and first-responder clients, but as we discussed in Chapters 2 and 3, their stress response systems don't know it. They are responding, drop by drop, as if their life or limbs were at stake. This is how the ANS functions. Without awareness and the skills to allow the ANS to recover, they are in danger of burnout and very possibly serious illnesses.

In this chapter, I present two case studies of individuals from demanding professions, not in the life-or-death way, but in the more common way: long hours, long weeks, and limited resources to manage the load. The two individuals I will introduce appear to work very different jobs, but fundamentally, they suffered in the very same way. One is a public school teacher, and the other is a supervising officer who works with individuals accused of crimes who haven't yet been convicted.

These two examples of dedicated servants face mental and physical health risks that are due to the chronically challenging context of their careers. Unlike first responders in the military, they don't go through Stress Inoculation Training, nor do most of them enter the field aware of the level of threat. My work with them, and hundreds like them, is to offer them an opportunity to stop the drop-by-drop stress accumulation and enhance their interoceptive awareness in order to allow their nervous systems to fully recover.

ALICIA, PUBLIC SCHOOL TEACHER

Let's start by looking at the "drop-by-drop" situation of a teacher from a large K-12 public school system in the U.S. who serves a significant student population from disadvantaged communities. The teachers and administrators here face particular challenges, including chronic underfunding (many teachers buy their own classroom supplies), students from unstable home environments (and other challenges that get in the way of their learning), subsequent behavioral issues in the classroom, and safety concerns. On top of all these challenges, these teachers care a great deal about their students, which adds an additional layer of emotional and psychological stress.

I had a conversation with a group of K-12 teachers toward the end of their school year. I began the workshop by facilitating a discussion about their sources of joy, successes, and challenges. After talking about the good stuff, I asked them to share their biggest stressors. Alicia, a sixth-grade teacher, said, "It has been a rough year, but mainly I'm worried that my kids won't eat during the summer or that they won't return to school next year." She went on to explain that many of them live in very dangerous neighborhoods with parents who are absent most of the day and night. "So yeah, I worry about gang activity, shootings, and if they're even going to be able to eat."

As a group, we talked about these concerns, as well as their daily workloads that extend well beyond learning-based tasks. They comfort students, de-escalate behavioral crises, meet with parents (or try to), and constantly work to keep their students engaged despite their exhaustion. Forget self-care for these teachers. So much energy goes to their students that there is barely anything left over for their own families.

PROBLEM

This unrelenting stress had been manifesting itself physically, leading to symptoms like frequent colds, infections, digestive-system issues, elevated blood pressure, headaches, and brain fog. Despite dealing with these health-related challenges, Alicia and the other teachers continued to drive on because of their commitment to their students' needs.

Alicia told me that her colleagues and principal had commented on changes in her behavior, such as mood swings and isolation from her peers. While she knew something was wrong, she couldn't imagine letting up the pace for one moment, much less a day. When we met one-on-one, she was seriously contemplating leaving the teaching field after a ten-year career. This brought her a lot of sadness and guilt that she would be abandoning the kids who needed so much help.

SOLUTION

Following the initial four-hour workshop, I worked individually with Alicia. As is typical for people who have severe symptoms, they are motivated to do something but are still stuck in the high-op-tempo world that got them there. They have a very difficult time finding time to do what is necessary to get them back to a healthier place.

Additionally, they are so accustomed to operating in a chronically stressed state that it almost feels uncomfortable to have a regulated ANS. So, we moved slowly and started creating a habit of integrating body-based self-regulation into her day. Alicia was well aware of bodily sensations and seemed to understand what they were telling her if she stopped and reflected. I built on that capacity by guiding her in formal mindfulness practices, which she integrated into her daily routines. She kept a journal that tracked her bodily sensations, thoughts, moods, and energy levels, which helped reinforce her interoceptive awareness and improved her capacity to take time, even ten minutes throughout the day, to regulate her mind and body.

OUTCOMES

By the end of the summer break, Alicia had incorporated physical exercise and yoga into her routine. She was able to bring her blood pressure back to normal without medication, her digestive issues disappeared, and her headaches became infrequent even into the next school year. She rekindled relationships with her peers and some friends that she had neglected in her personal life. Her family even commented that she seemed happier and was more patient. Today, she is still teaching and loves her job.

CECILIA, FEDERAL SUPERVISION OFFICER, U.S. COURTS

Let's take a look at Cecilia, who for 15 years has worked as a federal supervision officer in a large U.S. city reentry court. She and her team have three main areas of responsibility:

1. Monitoring clients who had been released and were pending trial
2. Overseeing clients sentenced to probation
3. Supporting clients who were reentering the community after being released from prison

The job requires them to strike a balance between enforcement and rehabilitation, protecting public safety while helping clients reintegrate into society and rebuild their lives.

Cecilia managed a large caseload of individuals with complex challenges, including addiction, homelessness, mental health issues, and a pull back to criminal connections. She and her team were trained through the Staff Training Aimed at Reducing Re-Arrest (STARR) program. This cognitive-behavior-based program is designed to help supervising officers more effectively engage with their clients to change thinking patterns that contribute to criminal behavior.

PROBLEM

I have chosen to focus on Cecilia's challenges as an illustration of those generally experienced by the rest of the team.

Despite Cecilia's dedication, her caseload and burdensome administrative demands wore her down. She felt that her work life was like a yo-yo, with success one week and setbacks the next. She also dealt with vicarious trauma after hearing story after story of her clients' experiences of abandonment, violence, drug abuse, and outright despair. In addition to all of this, she had two children in primary school and lived far from her family, so she had few child-care options. She was exhausted, emotionally and physically.

When I started working with Cecilia and her team, she had been experiencing numerous symptoms for almost a year, none of which she associated with stress. She knew she was tired all the time, but wasn't aware of the toll that her workload was taking. In our one-on-one sessions, she talked about having persistent headaches, difficulty sleeping, and emotional exhaustion, with little energy left for her husband and children. She found herself zoning out in meetings, omitting key details from her reports, and feeling detached from her clients. This created further distress because, while she cared, she didn't have the emotional bandwidth to deal with all of their challenges.

Cecilia's team described her as being increasingly disengaged and indifferent, which was out of character. They talked about her withdrawing from team discussions, staying quiet during case-review meetings, and becoming more reactive to minor frustrations and normal inter-office conflicts. They interpreted her behavior as a lack of commitment or carelessness, saying she seemed burned out.

Distrust was developing between Cecilia and the rest of the team. Although she felt she was doing her best, frustrations and misunderstandings started to chip away at their overall team cohesion. Problems were also developing between Cecilia and her supervisor, and the tension grew when Cecilia received her annual review, during which her supervisor questioned her effectiveness and how much she still cared about the job.

Cecilia left the review feeling completely misunderstood and unsupported, which caused her to further isolate herself. The impact on Cecilia, her team, and her clients was significant.

SOLUTION

I was brought in to deliver a day-long workshop, followed by individual coaching, to help Celia's team improve their ability to support change in their clients. I was asked to help them further develop skills in social and emotional intelligence, improve decision-making in complex situations, and work on stress management. The coaching aimed to strengthen the abilities of a group of about twenty supervising officers in four key areas, which are the goals of the STARR program:

1. Helping clients understand expectations
2. Balancing fairness and accountability
3. Teaching structured decision-making skills to clients
4. Providing reinforcement and corrective feedback based on client behavior

I asked about any metrics related to the success of the STARR approach, looking for particular areas that needed reinforcement or additional skills. What became clear during the workshop was that, while STARR had been proven to help address risk factors for future crime, it was as effective as the person managing the conversation: the supervising officer. That effectiveness came down to their stress management.

This realization, along with others during the workshop and the upcoming STARR refresher, gave us a golden opportunity to look at the skills they relied on most to help their clients. We were able to separate the discrete cognitive-behavioral techniques of this program and reinforce their internal capacity to use them with clients.

They had never heard of interoception, much less interoceptive awareness, and were fascinated by its role in just about every aspect of functioning. Some struggled more than others with building awareness of internal bodily sensations, but they all worked at it. Between the workshop and the follow-up coaching, each improved their ability to sense when a stress response was happening, notice what was causing the stress, interpret bodily sensations in the context of the situation, and then regulate the stress level to the level needed for the performance.

We built on their improved interoceptive awareness to deepen their emotional and social intelligence skills and capacities (which they practiced at home as well). We conducted role plays to improve communication skills, boundary-setting, and self-regulation during tense interactions.

OUTCOMES

The team universally noticed after about two months of working together that they reached the end of their shifts less exhausted and felt more patient, attentive, and effective with their clients. They even felt comfortable talking to their clients about interoceptive awareness and teaching them some basic self-regulation techniques.

A post-survey showed that Cecilia, in particular, felt much better physically and was feeling more like her old self again with the team.

Through our training and coaching, Cecilia and her team (and leadership) came to realize that they needed more than a STARR refresher to be effective supervising officers for their clients. They needed to be sure they had the skills to self-regulate day by day, week by week, to use STARR to its full potential, and to maintain their own self-care.

INSIGHTS

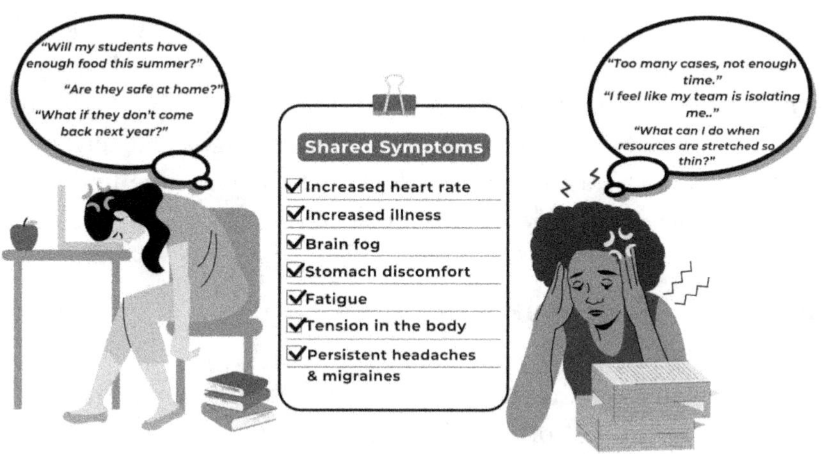

The bottom line is that the same chronic stress experienced by both Alicia and Cecilia can make even the most dedicated teachers and supervision officers appear disengaged. That can lead to misunderstandings, distrust, and a breakdown in team cohesion. Stress-related withdrawal is common, and it ends up creating a ripple effect, impacting not just individuals but the entire team dynamic. By incorporating interoceptive practices and stress-regulation techniques, we can all better sustain our energy levels and our engagement. It helps us improve communication within our teams and in other relationships, and it allows us to continue supporting those that we care about, all without risking burnout.

The brain-body system can only take so much before it breaks down. Those of us who dedicate our lives to serving others under stressful conditions deserve the tools to mitigate the health issues that come from these unrelenting high levels of stress. It helps us gain greater awareness that what might look like low morale, disengagement, lack of care, lack of team cohesion, and burnout is possibly the beginning of a silent killer.

If we can take moments to stop what we're doing to tune into the signals of the body and interpret them correctly, we create a whole new brain-body intelligence that will build our capacity to do anything we want.

The weak link lies with our capacity to fully utilize the tool. We should never assume that the tool or framework alone is all we need to manage complex situations, perform well, and maintain effective and meaningful relationships. If we're not managing ourselves and our stress, we can't assume the tool will get us across the finish line, no matter how many times we rectify or how many courses we take.

REFLECTION QUESTIONS

1. Do you track the effectiveness of human-development tools or frameworks you've introduced to your organization?
2. Can you imagine how your value can be impacted by the ability of your team to regulate their emotions and stress in the moment?

Chapter Nine

START-UP TO GROWN-UP: MAINTAINING CONNECTION TO VALUES

"It is not hard to make decisions once you know what your values are."
—Roy E. Disney

KEY TAKEAWAYS:

- Even positive stress (eustress) requires recovery. Without it, continuous demands can deplete resilience in individuals, teams, and organizations.
- We don't have to give up on a work cadence that is necessary to achieve great results; we must, however, give our system opportunities to fully recover (not just take short breaks).
- Chronic stress can lead to cultural myopia that narrows collective perception and focus, leading to a disconnection from shared purpose and core values.
- Interoceptive awareness helps individuals, teams, and organizations pause, reflect, and realign actions and decisions with core values and shared purpose.

It's easy to get lost in the demands of building a business and, in the process, become disconnected from ourselves and from the values upon which we created it. So, when I was invited to work with a fast-growing information technology (IT) startup, I wasn't surprised to find a convergence of these forces: the excitement of building something new, the drive to succeed against the odds, and the disconnection from core company values due to rapid scaling, growth pressure, and fatigue from a relentless pace. When we live with constant stress, even the kind of positive stress that accompanies the passion and excitement of growing a business, the price can be losing sight of elements (like company cultural values) that undergird the initial success.

This pulls away from our center bit by bit, and we lose touch with our integrity, our wholeness. This is relevant to interoceptive awareness in a couple of ways: (1) we make more decisions than many of us realize through gut-based wisdom, and living in our integrity is a felt sense, and (2) chronic stress, as we've discussed, tends to divert our attention away from the very thing that helps us sustain the energy needed to progress, heeding bodily signals that indicate a need for recovery and balance.

This next case study revolves around a young, international company founded on the values of team collaboration, collective and creative problem-solving, and risk-taking. In essence, one of the company's core principles in this example is psychological safety. It was how they launched and succeeded in the early period and how they believed they would become industry leaders.

PROBLEM

Growth brings opportunity, but it can also make it harder to stay grounded. John, one of the founders of this IT startup, reached out to see how I might help them with what he thought was either burnout or a deterioration of collaboration between departments in their small but growing company. He had been hearing about issues across all levels of the organization and across departments, from technical to finance to sales groups.

After talking with all the co-founders and department chiefs, I discovered that the company had experienced rapid growth in its lifespan of just over a decade. John talked about being proud of building the company from the ground up with a close-knit team that brought a particularly agile, can-do attitude to a fast-moving industry. As the company expanded, they got busy recruiting and did what seemed most important: hiring people with specific technical skills and IT-sector experience.

SOLUTION

It turns out, over the past few years, John and his co-founders had been so focused on establishing themselves as serious players in this well-developed sector that they weren't sure when things started to unravel. But it was becoming clear that innovation was stagnating, deadlines were being missed, and client engagement was declining. The board was worried about losing the market share that they had worked so hard to garner from more established companies. What also worried them was a sharp increase in the number of employees leaving for other companies early on.

They had the technical expertise to support the business, but it seemed that the ground underneath was starting to crumble. It was hard for them to pinpoint the problem or cause; they just knew that something needed to be fixed but were unsure what that was exactly.

My first task was to conduct an anonymous survey of employees to find out what might be underneath the symptoms that John described. I asked questions about teamwork and collaboration, workload and perceived stress, as well as potential burnout, comfort with bringing concerns to leadership, and transparency in decision-making. I also explored their perceived career paths and growth aspirations. I embedded questions designed to indicate their level of psychological safety, comfort with admitting mistakes (and viewing them as learning opportunities), willingness to take risks, ability to solve problems creatively, sense of empowerment to innovate, and so on. I also made sure the survey encouraged additional written feedback.

In addition to the confidential survey, I discussed hiring practices and talent management with the recruitment and learning and development teams. I wanted to find out what exactly they *thought* they were looking for in new employees versus what they might *actually* be looking for. For example, were they looking for people with personalities that fit the organization, or were they targeting technical expertise and experience? This discovery process was based on my understanding that the company branding emphasized technical expertise and reliability, along with an equally important factor of trust between the founders and the employees, *and* between the company and its customers.

I found out that trust and psychological safety were deliberate foundations of the company. Over time, it became an assumed value of the company rather than a practice. At some point during the transition from start-up to established company, hiring practices dropped as they considered how a candidate fit the company culture and values statement in favor of technical capabilities.

As the company expanded and hiring ramped up, no one thought to codify the company values and principles around psychological safety, trust, and what it takes to nurture and sustain team cohesion and strong customer relations.

Comments from surveys indicated that some employees no longer felt like it was the same company they had joined, the company environment felt toxic, new ideas were not welcomed, they had to cover up their mistakes for fear of reprisal, or they just didn't feel supported. I followed up on this survey through confidential one-on-one conversations with the employees. While the survey results did indicate, as John suspected, that employees were experiencing burnout, the follow-up, one-on-one discussions revealed less of a case of burnout and more frustration and stress due to what they felt was a tectonic shift in company culture and values. They felt betrayed, which created a big energy sinkhole.

It was time to take my discovery process to the co-founder and senior leaders. I shaped my questions based on the employee survey results and follow-up discussions. I then shared my overall observations, conclusions, and recommendations with the leadership team.

Based on the results from the survey and my discussion with employees and leadership, I recommended a two-day off-site retreat for top leadership and team leads. We used this day to revisit core company values and explore elements that foster collaboration, innovation, and motivation. We then dove into the important topic of stress and all of the intersection points between stress, performance, and growth potential for employees.

It often takes dedicated time away, like an off-site workshop, for people to actually embody new approaches to stress. As mentioned in earlier chapters, that word alone, "stress," tends to conjure up the idea of something we want less of, something undesirable. However, it doesn't actually take long for that knee-jerk perception to give way to a reminder that stress can be good and even helpful. I find that people like talking about stress, especially when there are opportunities for seeing it more honestly.

Interestingly, talking about stress tends to create a sense of community. It prepares a group for more awareness-building and creative problem-solving, looking at the relationship between stress as energy, team dynamics, and performance, as well as effective leadership. We engaged in activities that helped explain and explore how teams work and what makes them operate at a high level of functioning in a sustainable way.

We explored and experienced interoceptive awareness and how it specifically relates to cultural, social, and emotional intelligence. We conducted group exercises on what it means and feels like to live in our integrity, specifically reaffirming our individual and organizational values, what it feels like to live those values, and how we know when we start to stray from those values (to feel it in our bodies first, and then see it in our actions). We explored the research and practical understanding of the importance of psychological safety for high-performing teams.

The second day was devoted to integrating interoceptive awareness practices with scenario-based exercises, discussions, communication skills practice, and resilience building for enhanced performance. We wrapped up the retreat with a joint effort to create a company-wide plan to improve trust, collaboration, communication, and accountability.

Leadership agreed to offer one-on-one coaching sessions for employees as a follow-up to help them better understand and enhance their interoceptive awareness, stress regulation, and other skills to improve performance. We focused these one-on-one coaching sessions on interoceptive awareness practices and how those apply to their workday and, in fact, their personal lives. As I maintain, "everything affects everything," and John and his company agreed that an employee is a "whole person" showing up to work and wanted to provide tools to optimize that whole person. Seventy percent of employees opted for one-on-one coaching.

The company codified psychological safety as a cultural value, creating a simple, clear definition and embedding it in hiring, onboarding, and performance reviews.

We co-created a scorecard to be completed at 30, 90, 180 days, and one year, which helped assess their success in hiring people who were good matches for the company in both experience and values. They also implemented a values-based survey to keep a pulse on potential hot spots to address engagement and "belonging" factors of employees.

OUTCOMES

Six months after the retreat and following individual coaching, I conducted a follow-up survey and returned to lead a half-day session with leadership. The employee survey indicated a 68 percent overall improvement in psychological safety, job satisfaction, and morale. Through a combination of quantitative and qualitative measures, the company determined that innovation, collaboration, and customer engagement had improved significantly. Within six months, the company was heading back on track toward its targeted performance levels, both in-house and with its customer base.

INSIGHTS

As this case study illustrates, and as research supports, psychological safety is not just a nice-to-have component of the work environment. It's a cornerstone for healthy employee engagement; we might produce for a while under threatening and stressful conditions, but it won't last long. The company held this as a core value, but in their haste to increase market share and compete with larger companies, they overlooked what made them so successful.

In this case, it's not just a left-behind value. It's the nature of this value that was nearly devastating. As we have explored in previous chapters, when we do not feel safe, we enter survival mode. That's great when we're running for our lives, but not helpful when we need to engage our full range of intelligences: cognitive, emotional, social, and the insight that comes from accessing our body-based wisdom. When we access these capacities, we are not only performing at our best but are also healthier and happier, which feeds back into higher engagement, motivation, and performance. Chronic stress that stems from low psychological safety takes a toll on human resources.

When we can improve our interoceptive awareness, meaning that in any given moment we can tune into the body, notice what the body is telling the brain, insert ourselves into that conversation, and work to be part of the conversation by managing what's happening in the body and what's happening in the mind, we then can enhance our entire capacity. Improving this capacity improves many aspects of our performance and our psychological safety.

It helps us to self-regulate our stress response and our emotions. It enhances our empathy. It allows us to be more authentic, which leads to more social attunement and better relationships, and ultimately to stress resilience.

REFLECTION QUESTIONS

1. The next time you become aware that you do not feel comfortable in a situation or psychologically safe, take a moment to feel your body. See you if you can detect signals such as muscle tension, an increased heart rate, faster or shallower breath, and/or tightness in the throat or chest.
2. Also, try to check in with your body when you are feeling happy, comfortable, and safe. What sensations do you notice in the body in that state?
3. Can you imagine your organization integrating habits into its culture that enable everyone to access this important internal communication between the body and the brain?

Chapter Ten

EFFECTS OF DYSFUNCTIONAL LEADERSHIP

"It takes a remarkable fish to know it's in water."
—Unknown

KEY TAKEAWAYS:

- We can become so accustomed to unhealthy conditions that they feel normal.
- We can try to leave our problems at home, but we always carry our ANS with us.
- The health of our ANS will influence us everywhere we go, always.
- Even the most dysfunctional team can become functional if we address the underlying issues.

It's so easy to get sucked into the day-to-day without coming up for air to assess what kind of water we've been swimming in. How do we know when our situation has become unhealthy or dysfunctional? Whether this is the case with our families of origin, our close relationships, or our place of work, most of us go through life focused on achieving what is in front of us. Instead, we need to pause and take stock of our environment and context, and how that environment is helping or hindering our ability to achieve our goals and be the person we are capable of being.

The following case study highlights just how far things can go, how accustomed we can become to even severe dysfunction, and what it takes to realize the fishbowl we're in and how to clean it up.

Bill was the founder and president of a small but financially successful training company in a highly competitive sector. He was a retired military officer. He had a sharp business mind and was a creative thinker. We met at a training conference, and about a year later, he asked me to help his company enter the resilience-training space.

Bill's company generally had a headcount of about fifty people, many of whom had been with him since he founded the company twenty years prior. New people had been hired over time, and he enjoyed a retention rate of about ninety percent. On the surface, it seemed like a high-functioning organization. However, as I spoke with employees and looked into their company culture, experience base, and talent pool to determine what they needed to get into resilience training, I quickly picked up on an air of uncertainty, almost trepidation, in the office. Periodically, I would overhear people asking questions like, "Has anyone seen Bill or heard from him this week?" "How's Bill today?" "Did you finally get Bill's final revisions on the proposal that is due today?" and "Who is with Bill this time?"

PROBLEM

I had been meeting with employees for a few days when Bill came back to the office. His eyes were bloodshot, and he walked quickly to his office and slammed his door. I thought he must have pulled an all-nighter on the proposal and was tired and grumpy. He opened his door and yelled, "Clara, get me some coffee!" Clara jumped, gave her colleagues a look, and ran to the kitchen. He looked at me and said, "Colleen, can we talk?" As I entered his office and sat down, I noticed that he reeked of alcohol. Bill, as it turns out, pulled an all-nighter, but not to finish the proposal. He went on a bender. He apparently had a serious alcohol-use disorder.

What a situation! My impression, along with comments from his employees, indicated that Bill was a generous and kind-hearted man… when he wasn't drinking. What I discovered, however, is that his periods of sobriety lasted a month or two at best. During drinking binges, he would either try to attend all meetings (even with the customers) or hang around the office harassing people, sometimes yelling and saying very unkind things. The employees just shrugged their shoulders and said, "That's Bill." Despite the obvious impact of his drinking on all aspects of their work life, his words and actions were not taken personally by the employees.

Drinking or not, Bill demanded to be involved in every decision and to sign off on every purchase, even those under $25. To me, it seemed he was doing everything he could to maintain a sense of control, making up for the chaos he was experiencing internally. He had a very anxious management and leadership style, which was related to the dysregulation of his ANS.

Although he was known for being pretty unreliable, given his alcohol abuse problem, the employees he hired were very loyal. They covered for his inadequacies. They worked long days and long weeks to keep the company afloat. Interestingly, according to our discussions, it wasn't the financial rewards, love for their work, or the company's mission that kept people staying on for years (though Bill paid well). On the contrary, their constant frustration and anger stemmed from the need to cover for Bill, make excuses for him, and put in extra effort to manage the numerous tasks that fell through the cracks. This was made all the more difficult because he was in such high need for control, always causing delays. Micromanaging without reliability and follow-through had created enormous stress for his employees.

Why did they stay?

Bill knew what he was doing. He found people who were in difficult situations, working jobs that paid low wages and offered little respect. When he hired them, he saved them. They, in turn, saved him time and again. Bill had a very strong need for loyalty, which made sense given that he created such an unhealthy workplace. He also tended to find people who held porous or weak boundaries, both in terms of relationships and workload, very active antennae for anger in order to protect themselves, and a lot of practice at suppressing emotion. Simply, Bill's employees had the mindset and behavioral characteristics of adult children of alcoholics. Perhaps they grew up with a parent suffering from an addiction or experienced trauma in another form.

Whatever the background reasons for staying with Bill's company, discussions with staff showed they didn't realize the kind of "water" they'd been swimming in for many years. It felt normal, thus comfortable in a sense, to work in an unpredictable, unstable, unhealthy environment. It is what their ANS *knew* from previous experiences. Psychologists often say that people who move from one unhealthy relationship to another are used to that type of situation and treatment. I would make one change to that statement: the *ANS* of those of us who grew up with unhealthy behavior (instability, abuse, neglect, addiction, etc.) shows that we are accustomed to those conditions. As we have discussed throughout this book, the ANS underlies much of how we function.

Contrary to what many of us want to believe, we don't "leave our emotional baggage at the door." How is that truly possible? Even the fictitious characters in the hit Apple TV+ show *Severance* don't leave their nervous systems at home: although they may have severed minds, their bodies and nervous systems remain intact. We carry it *all* with us, *all the time:* brains, minds, and bodies. We may be able to box things up to some degree and for a while, but things have a way of leaking out. And Bill's childhood and military trauma weren't just leaking out; they were gushing.

While this case study is a fairly extreme example, as most companies are not run by alcoholics, employees go to work and bring their histories and "internal machinations." If there is chaos in our systems, it comes with us. Bill was a highly dysfunctional leader of a dysfunctional group of people, and the fishbowl was swirling with it.

I was very glad that they decided to expand their training to include resilience. Why? Because they needed their own level-up in resilience. They were plenty tough in their mindset, but as I've attempted to show in this book, being mentally tough is not the same thing as being resilient, healthy, and regulated. In fact, very often those who have survived trauma or adverse childhood experiences become stoic, mentally tough, as it were. This is a very effective coping mechanism, but it's not resilience, and it's not the same thing as being high-functioning.

SOLUTION

My first step was to help Bill and his employees become more aware of their environment by using the metaphor of the fish tank. I explained that their environment was like a tank with a water-circulation system (not filtration, mind you) that was much too powerful for the tank's size. It kept everything swirling, creating eddies everywhere, so there was never a moment when things were calm or the water was clear.

It took time to ease them into realizing the conditions that they had normalized. We discussed what happens to our internal functioning (our ANS) when we're living and working in an unpredictable and distrustful environment and how the brain-body system needs to constantly stay on alert because of that lack of predictability and safety. Thankfully, I had worked a lot with the U.S. military up to that point and was able to use a term that Bill, being former military as were most of his employees, would understand: "new normal." When service members deploy, a "new normal" occurs at home while they're away as their spouse or other family members take over their former tasks and responsibilities, and the same happens when service members return home.

With Bill and his people, we explored what new normal they desired, looking specifically at the bottom-line value of greater trust and psychological safety. Again, their normal modus operandi was some level of infighting (vying for Bill's approval) and one-upping each other in underhanded ways that made authentic team cohesion impossible. We went through exercises of what safety and trust feel like in the body versus the opposite. They were used to existing in a *Lord of the Flies* mode, but once they could conjure up times when they had been in a safe, trusting environment, they could sense it in the body and notice it in the mind.

Since this was an extreme case of working for years in survival mode, we spent most of our time building interoceptive abilities, learning to feel sensations in the body that were neutral or comfortable, in contrast to those present in fight-or-flight.

We met weekly in small groups to incorporate techniques that built interoceptive sensitivity and then worked to learn how to interpret those sensations accurately (moving them into the realm of interoceptive awareness). We continued with these sessions long enough for them to become habitual in their personal lives and at the office.

When we have been functioning at high levels of emotional stress for a long time, it is important to ease into interoceptive training. Some systems sense the effects right away, while some resist them for much longer. However, once the ANS starts to settle and become more regulated, this all clicks. It's as if the ANS says, *Ah, this is what I've needed all along.*

Bit by bit, over a few months, the employees became very attuned to their signature signs of an initial stress response and learned to regulate them for optimal functioning. They noticed less emotional reactivity (which isn't always becoming upset; it can also be shutting down and out, detaching, and dissociating). They saw how they thought quickly and clearly, and how they slept better. They communicated well, and interestingly, they set boundaries around Bill's behavior. Thankfully, Bill was more than ready and willing to do his own work.

Throughout this process, Bill and I had many honest conversations. He agreed to do coaching concerning the workplace conditions and to seek therapy with someone specialized in childhood trauma and addiction. I consulted with his therapist so that he could reinforce the interoceptive awareness I was teaching, and it was very helpful to their work. Interoceptive awareness prepared him for the therapists' focus on cognitive-behavioral techniques. I continued working with Bill and his staff for 6 months, providing group training and individual coaching.

OUTCOMES

I'm happy to report that Bill and his entire staff are doing well today. As of this publication, Bill has been sober for two years, and every single member of his staff is still with the company, some having entered into their own therapy, and all of them having found a new normal in how they manage their daily stress, team cohesion, and effectiveness. Bill slowly learned to delegate more to the senior staff members, who execute duties to perfection.

The company has grown in employee count and has indeed moved into the resilient sector, even helping others improve their own resilience.

A growing body of research is currently looking at interoceptive awareness for a number of challenges, including addiction, depression, anxiety, and eating disorders, among others.

INSIGHTS

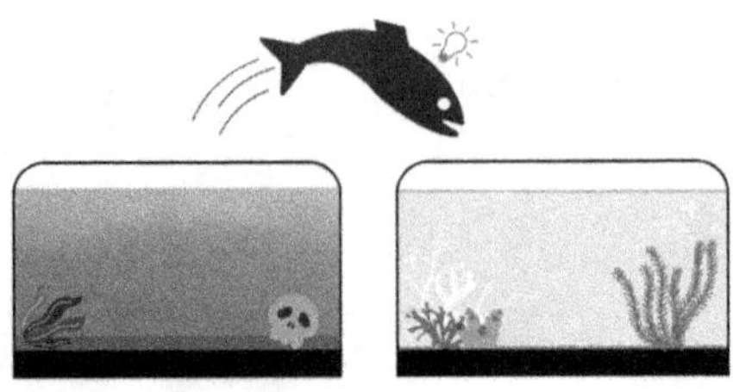

We often like to kid ourselves that we check our emotional selves at the door. But the truth is, those emotions, fears, and insecurities have a way of sneaking out when we least expect them. It takes a remarkable fish to know it's in water. And my goal is to help every "fish" out there identify what kind of water it's swimming in and make better decisions about how to improve its own response to its environment. We only have control over ourselves, but there's incredible power when team members, together, choose to change and swim in unison.

REFLECTION QUESTIONS

1. Do you have behavioral patterns or habits at work that resemble those in your personal life? Would you like any of those patterns or habits to be different?
2. What type of inappropriate behavior do you excuse? How does that serve you to excuse them?
3. Do your personal values align with those of your workplace? How does this alignment or misalignment affect you?

Chapter Eleven

THE GOLDILOCKS PARADOX

"Knowing yourself is the beginning of all wisdom."
—Aristotle
"Excess is similar to deficiency."
—Confucius

KEY TAKEAWAYS:

- It is important to know how to increase your stress level, not just how to decrease it.
- Modulating our stress to a "just right" level that fits the task or situation goes a long way toward sustaining our well-being and performance.
- The more we practice modulating our stress level, the easier it gets.
- Sufficient stress isn't just good for performance; it can be critical for safety.

The previous case studies were examples of too much stress for too long, with little to no awareness. As we know, stress is neither good nor bad; it is just a natural response to a perceived or real challenge or threat. What makes it good or bad, positive or negative, helpful or harmful is partly determined by how we view the challenge (stressor), how we respond to it, and, very importantly, how we recover. It comes down to having the right level of stress, using it, and recovering.

There are times when we need more stress in our system, i.e., up-regulate, so that we can have the necessary level of alertness, focus, and engagement to think clearly and make appropriate decisions. This, interestingly, is something many of us need to learn to do, but first, we need to know how to determine if we have the right level of stress. That's where knowing ourselves is key. By paying attention to how stress shows up for us (first in the body, then in the mind, and lastly in behavior), how we perform under a given level of stress and what it feels like, and how we recover and what that looks and feels like, only then can we truly understand our patterns.

In this final case study, I will share an example of the tricky paradox of stress, highlighting when too little stress is dangerous in the short term and too much stress is dangerous in the long term. We'll look at how interoceptive awareness helped them address the risks of their profession at both ends of the stress-performance scale.

JUST RIGHT!

Let's return to the illustration from Chapter 1 of the relationship between stress levels in our brain-body system and our performance. This U-stress curve helps emphasize stress as energy and our ability to intentionally modulate its level to reach our (individual) *sweet spot*, or optimal performance zone.

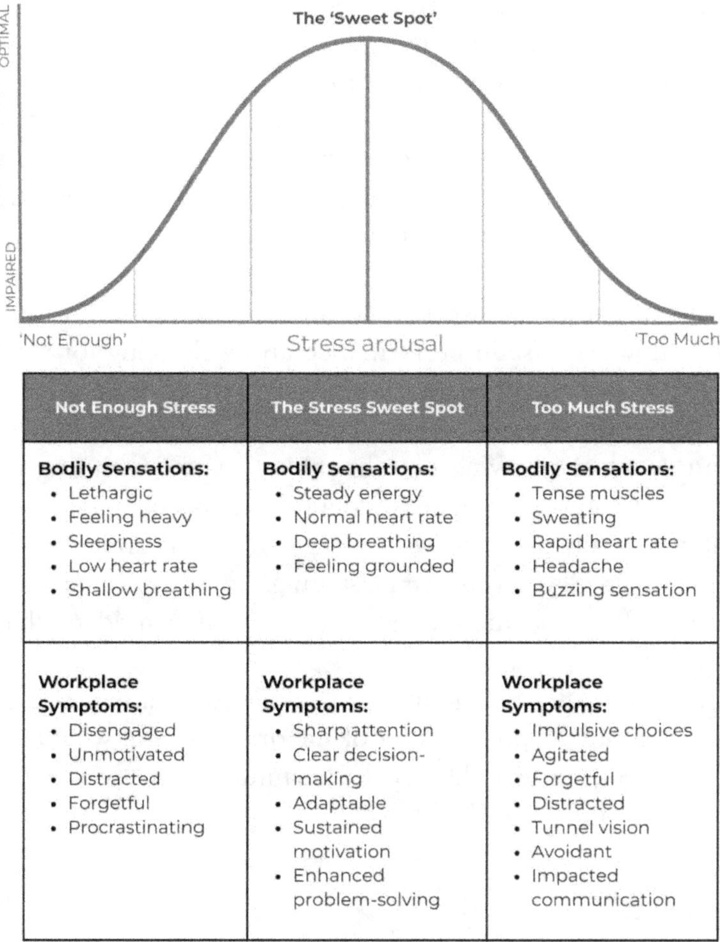

Not Enough Stress	The Stress Sweet Spot	Too Much Stress
Bodily Sensations: • Lethargic • Feeling heavy • Sleepiness • Low heart rate • Shallow breathing	**Bodily Sensations:** • Steady energy • Normal heart rate • Deep breathing • Feeling grounded	**Bodily Sensations:** • Tense muscles • Sweating • Rapid heart rate • Headache • Buzzing sensation
Workplace Symptoms: • Disengaged • Unmotivated • Distracted • Forgetful • Procrastinating	**Workplace Symptoms:** • Sharp attention • Clear decision-making • Adaptable • Sustained motivation • Enhanced problem-solving	**Workplace Symptoms:** • Impulsive choices • Agitated • Forgetful • Distracted • Tunnel vision • Avoidant • Impacted communication

Figure 11.1: Introceptive Stress-Performance Curve (adopted from Yerkes-Dodson, 1908)

At low levels of stress, we're not focusing, paying attention, or feeling engaged or motivated. As stress increases, we move closer to an optimal level, the top of the inverted U-curve. Some call this the "flow state," when time seems to slow as we execute a move or an intellectual feat nicely. This is when we have just the right level of challenge for our skill set and when we're highly motivated and focused. As our stress activation goes up, we will eventually start falling off the top of the performance curve and experience distress.

Interestingly, and relevant to the goal of understanding how our level of stress impacts our performance, research has revealed that the same state, such as boredom or motivation, can occur at both the low end and the high end of the stress activation spectrum, all the more reason for us to be aware of our experience, physical, cognitive, and behavioral, so that we can better manage our performance conditions.

Finding the stress sweet spot (not too much, not too little, just right) is how we sustain performance and well-being for as long as possible. I suspect it's safe to assume that we have all had the experience of nodding off in class and then having the teacher call on us or of allowing our thoughts to wander during a meeting, only to have someone suddenly ask for our opinion. How about not realizing our eyes are glazing over until our partner suddenly asks, "Are you even listening to me?" All of these are examples of not having enough stress and then suddenly having a lot of stress.

These are attention-getting and sometimes embarrassing situations, but generally not a matter of life or death. But what about the times when it is, or could be, really harmful in some way to have too little stress in the system?

PROBLEM

A few years ago, I was asked to teach mindfulness to a long-haul trucking company that was very invested in maintaining its safety record and reputation for reliable on-time deliveries. They had heard that mindfulness is good for focus and attention, and leadership wanted to be sure they were doing everything they could to mitigate the risk of road accidents caused by drivers losing focus en route due to fatigue, sleep deprivation, and other health conditions.

The statistics on long-haul trucking accidents due to driver fatigue and distractions are well-documented. Even with laws restricting driving hours, drowsy driving is a huge risk because of the pressure to fulfill delivery deadlines, and, let's be practical, good safety records also mean lower insurance costs.

As I started my inquiries to figure out the best way to approach this request, it became clear that before we could get to mindfulness, we needed to increase their interoceptive awareness. I have found that it can take quite some time for people to see the benefits of mindfulness, but there is a way to prepare.

I wanted to first get them to a reasonable level of knowing how to regulate stress in their ANS, whether that be to increase it (to be more alert and focused) or to decrease it to allow them to fall asleep and stay asleep the necessary number of hours. I wanted them to be able to regulate their energy level without relying solely on caffeinated drinks or smokeless tobacco.

We also needed to address the stress caused by the job and delivery pressures, as well as the internal and chronic stress that comes from sitting too long and having a sedentary lifestyle.

SOLUTION

I started them off with an initial four-hour in-person session as a large group. As always, we did a deep dive into the topic of stress: what it is, how to recognize our signature signs of stress right as they start, and how to get to know ourselves so well that we could quickly determine if our stress activation is too low, too high, or just right. It takes some time to learn what those levels feel like in the body and how they manifest in our mental state and behavior.

We've talked about how to manipulate the level of stress in our system (how to lower it when it's too high and increase it when it's too low), like when we're feeling lethargic or distracted when we need to be focused.

I explained that the best way to get to know how to manipulate their brain-body system is through interoceptive awareness. I taught them how to tune into their bodies to become aware of the signs of stress and how to modulate them, like how they manipulate the gas and brake pedals.

They certainly knew what it was like to feel drowsy behind the wheel, to have foggy thinking and slow reaction times. They hadn't, however, linked it to stress. Like most people, they thought about stress as a bad thing. By the end of the first in-person session, they were much more familiar with their minds and bodies. They were able to recognize and log how stress showed up for them.

I emphasized the importance of becoming so tuned in that we can, in any moment, quickly assess our stress level and decide whether it's at the right level. We practiced neurophysiological self-regulation techniques to raise and lower their stress level and other movement and mental techniques to inject energy into their systems.

In our initial sessions over a period of four weeks, we practiced using interoceptive awareness to make choices that helped them reach their goals. For six weeks after, we moved into traditional mindfulness practices.

During the time that we were integrating mindfulness, we dove deeper into other issues they face in their profession. One of my favorite phrases is "everything affects everything," and this was never more true than for truckers, who sit for long periods.

As a group, we explored what it's like for them to sit for these long periods. Some described tight shoulders and back or a sore (or numb) rear end. But that's only the beginning. We talked about how sitting for extended periods causes an imbalance in our brain-body system. It leads to chronic inflammation, compromises our immune system, and disrupts our biological energy system, which raises the risk of heart disease and diabetes. It also throws off our natural sleep-wake cycle, as well as the hormones that help us feel tired when we need to sleep and alert when we need to pay attention. Lack of movement over time can diminish our brain health and wreak havoc with our moods, even leading to depression and/or anxiety.

We can see that just looking at one requirement for the job, sitting for long periods, has a number of downstream effects on our brains, our minds, and our bodies. It certainly makes it difficult to stay alert, and yet, it leads to a number of other issues that exacerbate the problem of drowsiness. Everything affects everything, especially in this case.

So while the company wanted me to address drowsiness, it was important for us to talk about what actually leads to drowsiness besides sitting in a truck for hours upon hours.

Let's explore a couple of examples of how everything is interconnected. Have you ever noticed how, after a bad night's sleep, you're hungrier than usual? And, let's be honest, we're not usually hungry for a salad after a bad night's sleep. We crave something that we know isn't good for us, something greasy or high in processed sugar. So, poor sleep leads us to crave junk food, and it messes with our hunger hormones. It throws off our hunger signals, slows our metabolism, and leads to weight gain.

Now we've got weight gain, and guess what? That impacts all of the things above, including sleep apnea. Weight gain is one of the biggest factors in developing sleep apnea. Sleep apnea leads to worse sleep. Worse sleep leads to more drowsiness behind the wheel.

So, we looked at eating habits, sleep, and all the rest. And very importantly, I told the group the same thing I tell every group: while the techniques and practices I share are relatively simple, they are not necessarily easy. They need to be practiced with patience and kindness toward ourselves, and they need to be practiced consistently.

Nothing about this is a quick fix. It takes time and effort to get to the point where the techniques, tools, and approaches are effective. It takes time and effort to create new habits.

This is where the next phase of my work came in. After the team sessions, I provided one-on-one coaching to focus on specific areas of concern for each of them, including their goals for better health and their relationships back home.

OUTCOMES

I sent questionnaires at various intervals of our training and coaching that included write-in sections for qualitative feedback.

The questionnaires looked at lifestyle habits, mood stability, relationship quality, and drowsiness during hauls.

Six months after the training and coaching sessions, sixty-seven percent of the truckers reported experiencing more even energy levels on the road and at home; seventy percent had better quality and longer periods of sleep at home and on the road; forty-eight percent had lowered their blood pressure without medication; fifty-nine percent had reduced their alcohol use at home and reliance on tobacco to stay alert on the road; and fifty-two percent had lost at least eight pounds.

They reported catching their urges to text when driving. (Even though it is against company policy, they admitted to doing it, as most of us do despite laws against it.) They were better able to redirect their minds when their attention wandered off while driving and while talking to their spouses and kids. They even found that it was easier to redirect negative thoughts to more positive ones.

The trick is catching urges and resisting them. Awareness of an urge and the ability to resist are always outcomes of enhanced interoceptive awareness, especially when followed by mindfulness practice.

INSIGHTS

I'd like to bring it back to the Viktor Frankl quote mentioned in the introduction: *"Between stimulus and response, there is a space. In that space is our power to choose our response. In our response lies our growth and our freedom."*

Our human capacity to create space between stimulus and response is very powerful, as this quote says. However, we can't fix what we can't see. This is the amazing potential of interoceptive awareness training and coaching, especially when it's coupled with mindfulness techniques. Only what we pull out of the shadows and into the light can we truly change.

REFLECTION QUESTIONS:

1. When have you found yourself to be complacent, and what does that look and feel like?
2. What benefits might result from an ability to dial up and down your stress level at will?
3. Would you like to be more responsive and less reactive? If so, in what areas of your life?
4. How can creating space between an event and your response help you?

Conclusion

We're all students of human nature from birth, watching, inferring, and learning even when we don't realize it. When my mother remarried, I was two and a half. I watched how my stepfamily treated my brother and me as outsiders to their established tribe. Somehow, my observations taught me which behaviors would earn acceptance and love from my new father and siblings. My life became easier than my brother's. Two years older and full of anger, he couldn't (or wouldn't) adapt the same way.

I was far too young to have a conscious memory of those calculations. But the outcomes are clear: I found my way into that family; my brother never did. Somehow, I'd learned to read social dynamics and adjust accordingly, securing what all children need most: the safety of belonging.

I make this retrospective assessment of what I did as a toddler based on a fascinating book, *Scientist in the Crib* (Gopnik, Meltzoff, and Kuhl 1999), which I came across about twenty-five years ago. The book explores how we, as babies, keenly observe the world, make inferences, and run our version of experiments. While the authors focused on how we use these capacities to learn about the physical world, we also construct theories about our social world, particularly about relationships and getting our needs met. We are biologically wired to learn through our caregivers, which is aligned with the theories of leading scientists in neuroscience, developmental psychology, attachment theory, and trauma research, whose work shows that early relationships strongly influence the wiring of our ANS and brain regions related to the regulation of stress, emotion, and other autonomic responses.

Given what I think was a predisposition to pay attention to what makes humans tick, it's not surprising that I eventually found my way from foreign languages and cultures (sidetracked by semiconductors and IT) to psychology to training and coaching and, finally, to this book.

My curiosity about human nature, how we respond in life, and how we learn continued to blossom as I aged and my experiences grew. I craved a deeper understanding of how we can get the most out of our capacities. When I learned two decades ago about interoception, I thought, "EUREKA!" I knew this was key to our functioning. Since then, I have devoured related research that, thankfully, is growing in this realm, expanding now to an understanding of not just how this natural process unfolds between the body and the brain, but also how we can be part of that process, thereby enhancing its benefits.

While much of the literature still focuses on interoception (the natural, ongoing process), more is emerging about interoceptive awareness, which underpins just about every human aspect of healthy functioning and is the part we can consciously improve. I am increasingly convinced that interoceptive awareness is the new frontier in our ability to enhance performance and well-being across all domains (social, cognitive, physical, and emotional/psychological in particular). At a minimum, it is a crucial part of the foundation we need to do our best without harming others. I believe that we can't be at our best and do no harm without awareness of our stress responses or the necessary skills to use them wisely and well.

My friend Zena Everett, author and speaker, writes in her book *Badly Behaved People*:

"What's crucial is how we react to pressure. Trying to protect ourselves from

it simply encourages behavior that upsets others and ignites the blue touch paper. It's easy to spot when people are behaving like idiots. And we can fall into the idiot trap ourselves. Can we change our behavior? Absolutely. Once we are aware of what we're doing, we can change."

I'd add one refinement to her final point: awareness of *what we're feeling and sensing in the body* makes change more effective. Real change begins with bodily sensations: the internal signals that communicate to the brain and guide how we think, make decisions, manage emotions, and connect with others.

We *must* start with the body. At the core of our functioning is our ability to "watch" our bodies as we move in and out of stress and use the resulting information to stay grounded, effective, and balanced. Humans are complex beings, and we approach every engagement and situation with a rich history of experiences. Many people imagine that their thoughts shape their lives, and they do, but it turns out that *how well we can feel and interpret what's happening inside our bodies* plays a powerful role in shaping how we think, how flexible we are, and how well we can shift perspectives when the moment calls for it.

No matter where we come from or where we live, our beliefs and perspectives are shaped by life experiences. But, as recent neuroscience shows, we are not prisoners of how our brains and nervous systems are wired. We have the power to rewire. We have more influence over our thoughts, our choices, and our behaviors than we realize. And because so much of how we think, decide, and respond is shaped by the ongoing conversation between brain and body, learning to understand that language is one of the greatest opportunities we have to grow into our best selves.

Interoceptive awareness is the first step in learning that language. It's how we begin to tune in, interrupt old patterns, and build a more flexible, grounded, and intentional way of being in the world.

I run a training program for groups to improve their interoceptive awareness, as well as a program to teach others to deliver this training internally to their organizations. If you're ready to integrate interoceptive awareness into your personal life, leadership programs, team development, or organizational culture, I invite you to reach out. This book and these trainings are my mission: to make interoceptive awareness an everyday term and to help each of us build this foundational capacity to improve our lives, our organizations, our families, and our societies.

I would be honored to support your organization in strengthening this inner capacity, which touches every aspect of our ability to thrive as the amazing human beings we are.

Acknowledgments

I know the proverb "it takes a village" gets overused, but it is the best way for me to capture how this book came to be. My village starts with my family: Ken, Maya, sisters, cousins, sisters-in-law, brothers-in-law, nieces, and nephews, and extends to the many friends across the globe who allowed me to bounce ideas off of them and then gave me their input on so many pieces. It extends to the thousands of workshop attendees, trainees, coaching clients, and colleagues who have trusted me enough to authentically share their struggles, journeys, and successes.

A particularly deep bow to Ken Mizuki, for his diligent attention to every chapter and for such valuable and honest feedback; to Maya Mizuki, my reliable sounding board, most insightful coach, and most ardent cheerleader (how fortunate to get all of that in a daughter!); and to Kelsi Gallagher, my right-hand person in a new business launch that accompanied the writing of this book. Kelsi willingly, enthusiastically, and skillfully donned many hats so that we could make it all happen. To DeAnne Bryant, who closely watched me suffer through all of the book iterations, listening to me go on and on during our long walks and hikes, offering input and solid support along the way. I am blessed by each of you and many more I don't have the space to mention by name.

Lastly, a huge thank you to all those who honored me with their endorsements and to the entire team at Game Changer Publishing for incredible patience and guidance, trying to keep me to a schedule, and showing empathy and support when I slipped!

This book is a labor of love. I could not have done this without all of you.

Thank You For Reading My Book!

As a thank you for buying and reading my book, scan the QR code below to access free interoceptive awareness resources or schedule a complimentary call to learn more!

Scan The QR Code:

I appreciate your interest in my book and value your feedback, as it helps me improve future versions of this book. I would appreciate it if you could leave your invaluable review on Amazon.com with your feedback.

Thank you!

References

Ainley, Josephine, Victoria Maister, Sophie K. Forster, Anne Pollatos, and Manos Tsakiris. 2014. "Bodily Focus and Emotional Cognition: A Possibility for Interoception." *Consciousness and Cognition* 26: 19–26. https://doi.org/10.1016/j.concog.2014.02.004.

Barrett, Lisa Feldman. 2017. *How Emotions Are Made: The Secret Life of the Brain*. New York: Houghton Mifflin Harcourt.

Barrett, Lisa Feldman, and W. Kyle Simmons. 2015. "Interoceptive Predictions in the Brain." *Nature Reviews Neuroscience* 16, no. 7: 419–29. https://doi.org/10.1038/nrn3950.

Bird, Geoff, Melissa Silani, Richard Brindley, Sarah White, Uta Frith, and Tania Singer. 2010. "Empathic Brain Responses in Insula are Modulated by Levels of Alexithymia but Not Autism." *Brain* 133, no. 5: 1515–25. https://doi.org/10.1093/brain/awq060.

Brooks, Jeffrey A., et al. 2017. "The Neural Representation of Emotion is Categorical." *Social Cognitive and Affective Neuroscience* 12 (10): 169–183.

Critchley, Hugo D., and Sarah N. Garfinkel. 2017. "Interoception and Emotion." *Current Opinion in Psychology* 17: 7–14. https://doi.org/10.1016/j.copsyc.2017.04.020.

Cui, Zeyu, Xuancheng Ren, and Jingren Zhou. 2025. "Semantic Engineering and Physiological Feedback: A New Frontier in Human-AI Interaction." *Journal of Advanced Computational Linguistics.*

Damasio, Antonio R. 1994. *Descartes' Error: Emotion, Reason, and the Human Brain*. New York: G.P. Putnam.

Dickerson, Sally S., and Margaret E. Kemeny. 2004. "Acute Stressors and Cortisol Responses: A Theoretical Integration and Synthesis of Laboratory Research." *Psychological Bulletin* 130, no. 3: 355–91. https://doi.org/10.1037/0033-2909.130.3.355.

Eisenberger, Naomi I., and Matthew D. Lieberman. 2004. "Why Rejection Hurts: A Common Neural Alarm System for Physical and

Social Pain." *Trends in Cognitive Sciences* 8, no. 7: 294–300. https://doi.org/10.1016/j.tics.2004.05.010.

Fermin, Catherine, Marisel Perez, Ariana F. Obee, and Katie C. Hart. 2024. "Benefits of Time Spent Outdoors in Early Childhood Education: A Systematic Review." *FIU Undergraduate Research Journal* 2, no. 1: Article 6. https://doi.org/10.25148/URJ.020107.

Frankl, Viktor E. 2006. *Man's Search for Meaning*. Boston: Beacon Press.

Füstös, Julia, Katrin Gramann, Beate M. Herbert, and Anne Pollatos. 2013. "On the Relationship Between Interoceptive Awareness and Emotion Regulation: Evidence from Event-Related Potentials." *Biological Psychology* 93, no. 1: 193–201. https://doi.org/10.1016/j.biopsycho.2013.01.012

Everett, Zena. 2024. *Badly Behaved People: How to Help Your Best People Survive Your Worst People*. London: Practical Inspiration Publishing.

Garfinkel, Sarah N., Anil K. Seth, Alice B. Barrett, James S. Suzuki, and Hugo D. Critchley. 2015. "Knowing Your Own Heart: Distinguishing Interoceptive Accuracy from Interoceptive Awareness." *Biological Psychology* 104: 65–74. https://doi.org/10.1016/j.biopsycho.2014.11.004.

Gluckman, Peter, and Mark Hanson. 2006. *Mismatch: Why Our World No Longer Fits Our Bodies*. New York: Oxford University Press.

Goleman, Daniel. *Emotional Intelligence: Why It Can Matter More than IQ.* New York: Bantam Books, 1995.

Gopnik, Alison, Andrew N. Meltzoff, and Patricia K. Kuhl. 1999. *The Scientist in the Crib: Minds, Brains, and How Children Learn*. New York: William Morrow.

Grabbe, Linda, Marianne Duva, and Nancy A. Nicholson. 2023. "The Community Resiliency Model®: A Trauma-Informed Approach to Building Resilience in Frontline Staff." *Nursing Management* 54, no. 1: 30–39. https://doi.org/10.1097/01.NUMA.0000904128.84755.20.

Levine, Peter A. 1997. *Waking the Tiger: Healing Trauma*. Berkeley, CA: North Atlantic Books.

Lieberman, Daniel E. 2013. *The Story of the Human Body: Evolution, Health, and Disease*. New York: Pantheon.

Kaufman, Scott Barry. 2013. *Ungifted: Intelligence Redefined*. New York: Basic Books.

Khalsa, Sahib S., Ralph Adolphs, Oliver G. Cameron, Hugo D. Critchley, Peter W. Davenport, et al. 2018. "Interoception and Mental Health: A Roadmap." *Biological Psychiatry: Cognitive Neuroscience and Neuroimaging* 3, no. 6: 501–13. https://doi.org/10.1016/j.bpsc.2017.12.004.

McEwen, Bruce S., and John C. Wingfield. 2003. "The Concept of Allostasis in Biology and Biomedicine." *Hormones and Behavior* 43, no. 1: 2–15. https://doi.org/10.1016/S0018-506X(02)00024-7.

McKinsey & Company. 2021. "'Great Attrition' or 'Great Attraction'? The Choice Is Yours." *McKinsey Quarterly*, September 8, 2021. https://www.mckinsey.com/capabilities/people-and-organizational-performance/our-insights/great-attrition-or-great-attraction-the-choice-is-yours.

Murphy, Jennifer, Richard Catmur, and Geoff Bird. 2017. "Classifying Interoception: Mechanisms, Assessment, and Selection." *Neuroscience & Biobehavioral Reviews* 80: 32–40. https://doi.org/10.1016/j.neubiorev.2017.07.002.

Newlands, Murray. 2024. *The Future of Authentic Leadership: Building Cultures of Belonging*. New York: Harper Business.

Pfeifer, Rolf, and Josh Bongard. 2006. *How the Body Shapes the Way We Think: A New View of Intelligence*. Cambridge, MA: MIT Press.

Porges, Stephen W. 2011. *The Polyvagal Theory: Neurophysiological Foundations of Emotions, Attachment, Communication, and Self-regulation*. New York: W. W. Norton & Company.

Sapolsky, Robert M. 2004. *Why Zebras Don't Get Ulcers*. 3rd ed. New York: Henry Holt and Company.

Schore, Allan N. 2001. "The Effects of Early Relational Trauma on Right Brain Development, Affect Regulation, and Infant Mental Health." *Infant Mental Health Journal* 22, no. 1-2: 201–69.

Siegel, Daniel J. 2012. *The Developing Mind: How Relationships and the Brain Interact to Shape Who We Are*. 2nd ed. New York: Guilford Press.

Solano Durán, Sandra, et al. 2024. "The Use of Interoceptive Awareness in Treatment of Psychiatric Disorders – A Scoping Review Protocol." OSF. August 13. https://doi.org/10.17605/OSF.IO/PXV5U.

Stark, Peter B., and Mary C. Kelly. 2016. *Why Leaders Fail: And the 7 Prescriptions for Success*. San Diego, CA: Peter Barron Stark Companies.

Tronick, Edward. 2007. *The Neurobehavioral and Social-Emotional Development of Infants and Children*. New York: W. W. Norton & Company.

Van der Kolk, Bessel A. 2014. *The Body Keeps the Score: Brain, Mind, and Body in the Healing of Trauma*. New York: Viking.

Wong, Simon. 2025. *Feeling Seen: The New Science of Empowered Teams and Shared Purpose*. Boston: Harvard Business Review Press.

www.ingramcontent.com/pod-product-compliance
Lightning Source LLC
LaVergne TN
LVHW010620100826
845148LV00014B/3053

* 9 7 9 8 9 0 1 5 8 2 0 2 2 *